# Hildebrand's Travel Guide

# KENYA

**Publisher**
K+G, KARTO+GRAFIK Verlagsges. mbH

Schönberger Weg 15–17
6000 Frankfurt/Main 90
Second Edition 1987
Printed in West Germany
ISBN 3-88989-068-7

**Authors**
Impressions: Reinhard Künkel
Information: Nana Claudia Nenzel,
Dr. Arnd Wünschmann, Dr. Angelika Tunis, Wolfgang Freihen

**Edited by**
Bernadette Boyle, Ellen Knutson

**Photo Credits**
Reinhard Künkel, Eckart Müller,
C. J. Eicke, NUR Touristic Service

**Illustrations**
Eckart Müller, Peter Rank, Manfred Rup

**Maps**
K+G, KARTO+GRAFIK Verlagsgesellschaft mbH

**Translation**
Darrell Charles, Dr. Arnd Wünschmann, Grace Meheran

**Lithography**
Haußmann-Repro, 6100 Darmstadt

**Type Setting**
LibroSatz, 6239 Kriftel

**Printed by**
Schmitt+Läufer, 6300 Gießen

## Contents

2

3

4
5

6
7

9
Sixeighty
Hotel
DATA CENTRE

10
11
12
13

15

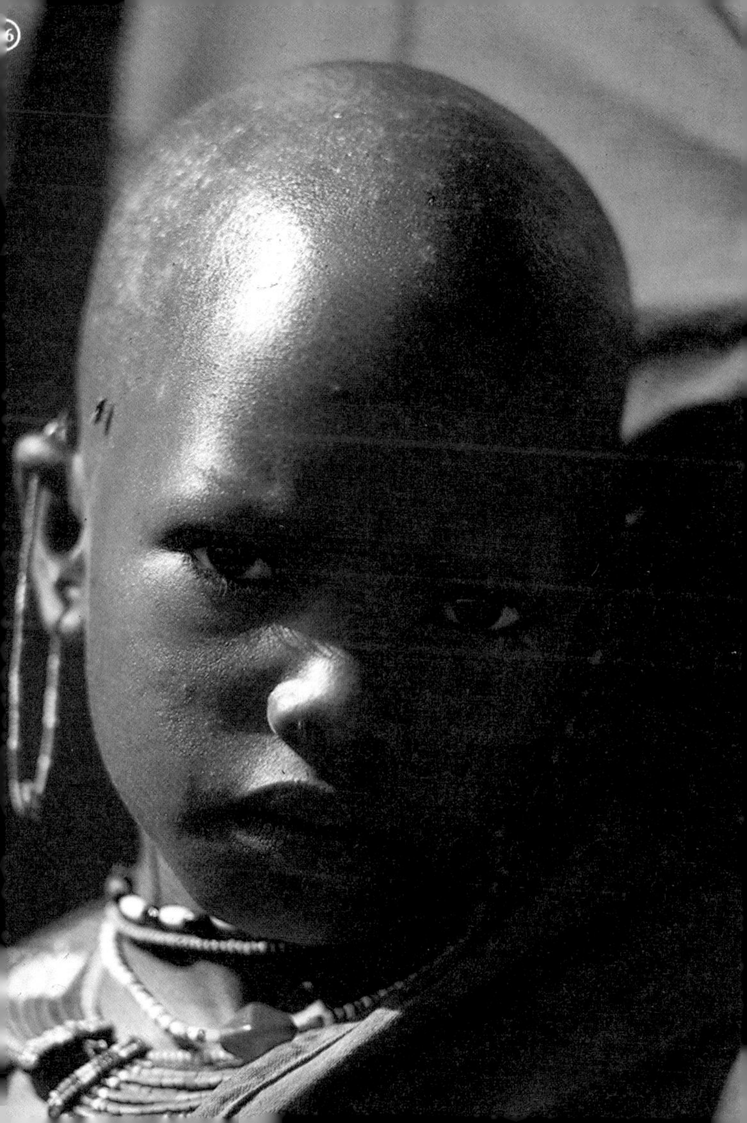

17

18
19
20
21

24

25
26
27
28
29
30

33

34

35

36

37

38
39

41

# Captions

**1.** The four gigantic elephant tusks over Moi Avenue (Kilindi Road) have become the symbol of the port of Mombasa.

**2.–5.** Richly-carved doorways (2) and ancient canons along the harbour (3) are reminders of Lamu Island's Arabian past, as are the dhows, barges and fishing boats with their triangular sails (5) which still ply the East African coast. The inhabitants of Lamu come from many different racial backgrounds.

**6.** Spurges (here, Euphorbia candelabrum) and other undemanding plants have gradually gained a foothold in the still fresh lava of this volcano in Tsavo Park. The volcanic nature of the land has left its mark on Kenya's landscape in the mountains...

**7.** ...and in the African Rift Valley, which, with its 1,000 m high, sheer walls and its lakes and savannas of the wide valley plains, is at its most impressive here.

**8.** Kenya's sunshine coast with its marvellous white sand beaches is protected from strong surf – and from sharks! – by the coral reef.

**9.** Kenya's capital, Nairobi, consists not only of modern, high-rise buildings but also of sprawling slum areas in the outlying districts.

**10.–13.** 48 different tribal groups make up the people of Kenya. Tribal feuds are now a thing of the past and the various groups are unified under the motto "Harambee!" (Let us come together and work together). The Turkana (10) and Samburu (11) in the north are Nilo-Hamitic pastoral nomads. Arabs (12) live as craftsmen, merchants and fishermen on the coast. Among the Bantu tribes, the Embu and Meru (13) are known for their tradition of music and dance.

**14.** Mosque in Nairobi.

**15.–16.** Magnificent glass-bead neck ornaments in tribal colours are the pride and joy of the Masai women.

**17.** Masai warriors in front of a low communal hut made of branches, cow dung and loam. Their hair is dressed using animal fat and coloured with ochre.

**18.–21.** All the fruits of the land are to be found on sale in Kenya's village markets. Craftsmen sell carvings and woven goods, providing reasonably-priced souvenirs for the visitor.

**22.** Perch and catfish, the two most important food fishes from the rivers and lakes, are laid out to dry after the catch is brought in.

**23.** Coastal fishing in the traditional dhow.

**24.** African buffalo and zebra at the water-hole in front of Kilaguni Lodge (Tsavo Park). Animals even appear here in the middle of the day to bathe and drink.

**25.** The crowned crane with its occipital tuft of bristle-like feathers.

**26.** A brown-headed kingfisher. There are many different species of kingfisher present in East Africa.

**27.** The secretary-bird, one of the most remarkable birds of prey in Africa, has an unusual crest of long, quill-like feathers.

**28.** A red-billed hornbill, a small hornbill commonly found in thornbush and savanna regions of Africa.

**29.** A golden weaver-bird building its nest.

**30.** A griffon vulture taking a sun bath with outstretched wings.

**31.** With the exception of during the breeding season, ostriches live in large flocks.

**32.** Crowned cranes alighting on a tree at sunset.

**33.** Thousands of flamingos on and around a crater lake on the edge of the Rift Valley. Such lakes, the waters of which are rich in soda, provide the flamingos with a nesting place and with the algae on which they feed (and which they filter from the water using their highly specialized beaks).

**34.** Bright red beaks and legs and the deep pink colouring of their plumage characterize the lesser flamingos of East Africa. Nowhere else can they be found in such great numbers.

**35.** The mating season is a time of fierce fighting among rival zebra stallions.

**36.** Elephants need close bodily contact with each other. With trunks entwined, these elephants engage in playful wrangling.

**37.** A pride of lions taking their daily rest on rocks above the grassy plain.

**38.** During migration in the rainy season thousands of gnus and zebras cross rivers in flood. Many do not survive the crossing.

**39.** Black rhinoceros mother with her calf; red-billed oxpeckers on her back and shoulders feed on parasites in the coat.

**40.** A cheetah after the kill.

**41.** Thorn trees (acacias) against the evening sky in the rainy season. Nesting marabou storks can be seen in the tree-tops.

# Nairobi

The Jumbo slid through the banks of fog like a ghost ship. Out of curiosity I stared into the fogginess outside my window which was sliced by the huge wing as if by a mighty sabre. I could see nothing – nothing at all. The pilot let himself be led by his electronic eyes through the clouds, which suddenly ripped open to reveal a green, rain-soaked steppe-like landscape. A few minutes later the huge bird landed and came to a standstill, trailing a white spray behind it. After an eight-hour flight through the night we had landed at the dawn of a grey rainy day at Nairobi's international Jomo Kenyatta Airport.

This hub of African air traffic, with its conglomeration of concrete blocks, luggage conveyor belts and aluminium profiles, differs in only one respect from other airports in the third, second or even first world: most jets take off and land at night or early in the morning, because – due to the great heat of the day – the air would then be too thin under the wings (Nairobi is 5,450 ft above sea level), which would mean reducing the payload. The half-hour drive from the airport into the capital took us through a grey, rain-veiled plain, from which the high-rise towers in the centre slowly grew.

Finally, we saw a sign saying "Nairobi – City in the Sun". However, that morning I found the original meaning of the Masai name to be much more accurate – it translates roughly as "cold swamp". It was precisely here that the builders of the railway line to Uganda (at the turn of the century Mombasa on the Indian Ocean was linked with Lake Victoria) erected the corrugated iron huts and tents of a big depot.

Within only a few decades that provisional railway workers' camp of those pioneering times has developed into an impressive metropolis,

whose skyscraper skyline seems alien to its African surroundings. The business lingo spoken in the city of Nairobi is understood much better in London or New York than in the "bomas" (only a few hours away by car) of the pastoral tribes who still keep to their traditional way of life.

The city centre, linked by modern communication means to other capitals and world trading centres, is a hive of hectic activity. The big multinational companies have branches here, just as banks, oil companies and airlines do. Every year, a number of international congresses and conferences are held in the Conference Center, which is equipped with all modern conveniences. In addition to numerous embassies and diplomatic agencies, various U.N. institutions underline the international importance of this East African capital.

Nairobi's main streets are full of people with differently coloured skins. Although most of them are of course Africans (mainly dark-skinned Kikuyus), people from all corners of the earth and of every imaginable colour of skin come together here where political and economic interests and strategies cross.

I welcome the opportunity to take a seat in the "Thorn Tree", which belongs to the traditional New Stanley Hotel, and observe, while drinking a cup of coffee, the passers-by. It's just like being in the cinema – only better. I note, for instance, the many different kinds of headwear: the skilfully wound turbans of the Indians, the fantastic hats of the streetwalkers decked out like birds of paradise, or the camel-leather stetsons of audacious holiday cowboys. Add to this the reflecting sunglasses and the brazen laugh of African gigolos.

Elegant Kenyans pass by in dark double-breasted suits, carrying an inordinately expensive diplomat's attaché case in their left hand and dangling a Mercedes key ring in their right. Then there are barefooted park boys, children and youths who earn a few coppers guiding drivers into parking lots and slipping apprehensively past the uniformed porter, a giant of a man well over 6 ft tall with a correspondingly weighty appearance.

In Nairobi, this centre of African belief in progress, you can buy everything which is made by traditional or modern manufacturing methods anywhere in this big country. In the souvenir and trinket shops you'll find pile after pile of fabrics, batiks, wood and soapstone carvings, masks, ritual objects, hunting implements, necklaces, bracelets, copper articles and all sorts of trash and bric-a-brac.

In Africa only the big shops have fixed prices; consequently, it is well worthwhile haggling with some degree of stubbornness over the price of any jewelry you have taken a fancy to, because the price initially stipulated by the seller is usually far in excess of what the article is really worth.

In addition to the luxury shops in the city centre, the small bazaar shops in Biashara Street are also a worthwhile shopping goal. And whoever likes the hustle and bustle ought not to miss just strolling through the big market hall, where nimble dealers offer, in addition to all sorts of other goods, a wide variety of exotic fruit and flowers.

If your safari programme leaves you a morning or an afternoon to spare, do at all events pay a visit to the National Museum, which has no end of extremely interesting objects on display from all periods of East African history; the prehistoric fossil collection is particularly famous, but the natural history exhibits are just as interesting. In the adjoining snake park you may get goose-flesh even on the hottest day if you suddenly find yourself observed by the lidless eyes of a green mamba, cobra or puff adder.

When strolling round town you should, however, not just admire the thousand big and small sights, but also be on the lookout for handbag snatchers, tricksters and black-market dealers who all too often take advantage, with consummate skill, of the inexperience or ingenuousness of tourists in order to make a quick buck.

For Nairobi is not only the multi-storey glass and concrete palaces of down-town, where numerous luxury limousines thread their way past exclusive shops in stop-and-go traffic – it is also a city of 850,000 inhabitants, far too many of whom live in the poorest of slums which, to make matters worse, turn into evil-smelling swamps in the rainy season.

Thousands of youths leave their native villages every year to seek their fortunes in Nairobi. Only a few find a job. All that is left for the others is the slums, where, caught between the pincers of unemployment and poverty, they simply live from one day to the next in conditions often unworthy of human beings.

The hardship existing in the plastic huts and cardboard shacks is a veritable breeding-ground for criminality and prostitution. The tourist living in the big hotels very seldom gets to see this seamy side of Nairobi, but may, if not too careful about his valuables, quickly make acquaintance with it if he suddenly finds his camera or traveller's cheques are missing.

The exciting nightlife of Nairobi also occasionally has its own kind of "wild life". Among the many pretty girls there are a few black mambas, whose bite is not necessarily lethal, but can have a long-lasting poisonous effect on one's wallet.

By the way, it is not the intention of these brief tips to sour your joy in getting to know Nairobi, but rather to help you experience more consciously the tingling atmosphere and vivacity of this fascinating multi-faceted city.

# Landscape, Flora and Fauna

The single engine of our plane hummed steadily. The compass needle pointed northwest. Maize fields unfurled several hundred feet below us.

Suddenly, the earth dropped away. We had reached the edge of the Rift Valley, the great African trough which extends like a long gash over the Earth's surface from the Dead Sea via the Red Sea and across East Africa down as far as Mozambique. In Kenya the rift walls sometimes reach a height of more than 3,000 ft, and the valley varies in width from 30 to 40 miles. In the basins of the valley the water has accumulated into lakes, the only freshwater lake, however, being Lake Naivasha.

The strong sunlight on the soda-rich waters of the other lakes produces ton upon ton of blue algae, on which flamingos feed. More than a million lesser flamingos have been counted on the shores of Lake Nakuru, straining the coveted material from the shallow waters through their sieve-like bills. These long-legged birds also inhabit the shores of Lake Bogoria, forming a broad pink-coloured ribbon which can be plainly seen from an aircraft even from a great height.

The Rift Valley area offers many sights of breathtaking natural beauty, which aren't in short supply in Kenya anyway. Although the equator passes through the centre of Kenya, the country's highest peak, Mt. Kenya (over 17,000 ft), has a snow and ice crown which doesn't melt even during the longest drought.

Kenya has almost everything in the way of scenic variety – from the moist savannas of the coastal zone to the semi-desert and desert near Lake Turkana – that Africa's landscape has to offer, including tropical rain forests and alpine zones.

As one would expect, the flora is just as extensive, encompassing a broad spectrum of species between the mangrove swamps of the coast and the giant lobelias on Mt. Kenya. During the rainy season wild flowers blossom and flat-topped acacias, the trees typical of the dry savanna, bloom; even the baobab trees, whose fruit provides sustenance not only for baboons but also elephants, are in blossom.

In some place there is absolutely no way through the hooks and thorns of a barrier of wild plant growth, and in others the wind tears the last tufts of grass from the bare soil and chases them like balls across the plain.

Palms and acacias, thorn bushes and desert roses, bamboo clumps and savanna grass – all of these and many more form the green backdrop for a magnificent animal kingdom which occupies every imaginable ecological niche offered by the vegetable kingdom.

It is only natural that the big animals are, initially, the most interesting: elephants, rhinoceroses, buffaloes, lions and leopards.

Rhinoceroses are unfortunately becoming scarcer and scarcer because of their horns, which play an important role as a raw material in traditional Asiatic popular medicine and which in the Yemen are made into dagger handles. In the last ten years 90% of the stock has been poached.

Leopards are also rarely seen, but this is because they are night prowlers. On the other hand, giraffes, gazelles and gnus are seen so frequently and you get so used to coming across them that you almost overlook them. Cheetahs, the long-legged sprinters among the wild cats, are also seldom seen, although they claim their prey during daylight hours. With a bit of luck and a great deal of patience, tourists occasionally manage to spot a cheetah, or sometimes several, on the hunt – a climax to any safari!

In addition to these well-known VIP's of the animal kingdom there is a great number of smaller creatures which, although they have no fiery mane or the yellow eyes of beasts of prey to advertise themselves with, can be just as interesting to observe as elephants, lions, etc. Most safari guests are so keen to discover a lion every day that their evening whisky just doesn't taste right if they don't.

Sometimes people tell me they've watched a lion taking an afternoon nap, and then they ask me if I've had a similarly exciting experience. When I then say I've spent all day watching "just" jackals, they frequently smile and feel sorry for me.

However, I find these little animals are also interesting in their way. This also goes for birds, lizards and insects, which can be found in great numbers on any safari.

Because of the population explosion and, as a result, the growth in the area under cultivation, big game is now found virtually only in the national parks and reserves. Each of these game reserves has its own character – from the point of view of either scenery or flora and fauna.

For example, the Tsavo National Park, Kenya's biggest, is famous for its red elephants. They are not really red, though – to care for their skin, the elephants plaster themselves with moist mud, which, when it has dried, hides the grey elephant skin under its red colour.

In the Samburu area, the narrow-striped Grevy's zebra (larger and more handsome than the common zebra found further south) and the reticulated giraffe are particularly conspicuous. It is also very easy here to observe the long-necked gerenuk antelope.

In the Masai-Mara Reserve bordering on Tanzania, huge gnu and zebra herds stream across from the Serengeti at certain times of the year. The Serengeti plain is also famous for its large prides of lions. In the Amboseli National Park, all wild life occurs below the snowy peaks of Mt. Kilimanjaro, at 18,000 ft Africa's highest mountain.

Wherever your safari takes you – whether in a rented car or a bus chartered by a tourist operator – experiences both commonplace and exciting will be waiting for you everywhere, and everywhere you may catch that medically undetectable but incurable Africa fever, which afflicts its victims all life long and forces them to keep on returning.

# Tent Safari

Night spread, soft as velvet, over the steppe. Only our campfire burnt a hole in the black curtain which seemed to hide all Africa's secrets. In the distance a jackal wailed, to be answered shortly afterwards from the other side of the night by a member of the same species. Suddenly a deep roar rolled through the scrub, silencing all other sounds. A lion, king of the animals, had unmistakably made his authority plain. With a few deep growls his threatening message finally ebbed, and was followed by an impressive silence.

Peter was the first to find his tongue: "I think he meant you", he said, grinning across at Charles,

at well over 200 lbs., the biggest man in our group. "For goodness' sake, don't say anything like that", Charles replied with a slight quaver in his voice, anxiously patting his not inconsiderable beer paunch. "I won't get a wink of sleep the whole night otherwise". As if to ban any further signs of danger, he took firm hold of his whisky glass and armed himself for all further emergencies with a big swig.

We were travelling in two Land Rovers. During the day we had been stalking elephants, buffaloes and rhinoceroses along the Mara River, and in the evening we pitched our tents under the widespread leafy canopy of a thorn tree.

Fried potatoes, beans and bacon were sizzling on the fire. The light from the flames caused restless shadows to dance through the camp. The heat of the day had given way to the pleasant cool of the evening. From a breathtakingly clear night sky the universe twinkled at us from a thousand bright eyes. And to round it all off, beer or whisky tasted like, well only as beer and whisky can taste after a hot, dusty day in the bush.

Tent safari – safari in its nicest, most original form – is an incomparable adventure which is worth taking upon oneself every day and every night anew. However, it is an adventure requiring enterprise, a talent for improvisation, a willingness to take risks, a joy of nature, and – last but not least – a fair share of dauntlessness. If you possess these useful characteristics, Kenya can offer you a number of holidays to your own individual taste.

In almost all national parks and wildlife reserves there are camping facilities, which cannot, however, be measured according to European standards. But, in return for being happy at having water and wood in addition to a lion's roar at your campsite, you don't have to share the latter with a thousand neighbours who build little fences round their tents; instead, you usually have the wide open steppe as your garden – completely for yourself. Tents and camping equipment can be hired in Nairobi, food and drink can be acquired in reasonably well stocked supermarkets, and the AA, the Kenyan Automobile Association, gives good tips and hints for the best spots and routes to them. You will also need a rented car, of course, if possible with a big boot or roof rack for the fairly extensive equipment. From my own experience I would urgently caution against starting your safari in the middle of the rainy season (cf. chapter on climate). Wet wood is so very difficult to set fire to, and on the third day at the latest even the most robust souls find it a bit difficult to consider it the done thing to run round in wet clothes.

By the way, bring your own sleeping bag from home, together with a torch and similar small items, which are often forgotten because they are thought unimportant, but which very quickly climb up the list of priorities when you're underway, particularly if you don't have them. After all, it is easier to open a tin of fruit salad with a tin-opener than with a bush knife looking more like a short sword, although you will still manage, as every old camping hand south of the equator knows only too well.

An essential part of your equipment should be a (full!) water canister – 20 litres if possible. It is precisely in the dry season that the distance to the next tap can be so far. And it does happen now and again that the car insidiously breaks down, and then you can congratulate yourself on having your own source in the canister.

Here is another tip garnered from my own safari experience: be sure to put food, half-full pots and similar remnants of your evening bush dinner in a safe place overnight, best of all in your car or tent, but at all events well out of reach of any four-legged neighbours. A hyena once stole half a chicken, which already had a firm place on the menu the next day, and the pot it was in, from the table. I found the pot the next morning a few hundred yards away – empty, of course.

Anyone who doesn't have the time to make the extensive preparations for such a trip himself can of course go on a tent safari with professionals. This is almost as much fun, but means a lot less work; is a bit less risky, but also costs a bit more.

At all events: Heia safari!

# Big-Game Hunting with the Camera

The two bull elephants entwined their trunks into a seemingly untieable knot, pushed back and forth with all their might, separated again, only to join battle again with their heavy ivory tusks clashing against each other.

As the backdrop for their gigantic duel they had chosen Mt. Kilimanjaro, whose snow-capped peak, like a reminder of a winter long ago, glinted in the evening sun.

The two giants could hardly have picked a more impressive backdrop for their exhibition, and the drumfire of clicking camera shutters emanating from a safari bus rolled accordingly. With an elephant, lion or rhinoceros in the viewfinder, the urge for most tourists to press the shutter-release is irresistible. The age-old hunting instinct erupts like lava and breaks through the thin surface of 20th century civilization and makes big-game hunters of even the most harmless nature lovers.

The animals, however, are in luck, because the only shots from most safari participants today come from telephoto lenses.

Before embarking on a trip to Kenya, many photo hunters make considerable additions to their photographic arsenal. And quite rightly so, because the lenses with the aid of which the Acropolis or the Leaning Tower of Pisa in all their beauty fill out a picture are hardly suitable when it comes to looking a cheetah or lion in the eye.

Animal photography is the classic field for the telephoto lens, and although you can get astonishingly close to the various animals in the national parks and game reserves, the distance is still in many cases too great to obtain satisfactory results with lenses of short focal length.

I would therefore recommend the more serious-minded photo hunter to take with him, as basic equipment, a single lens reflex camera, a 35 mm wide angle lens, a 135 mm telephoto lens and a long 400 mm zoom lens. This initial equipment may, depending on your interests and the state of your bank account, be expanded quite considerably. You should, however, put your equipment together in good time before you leave for Africa, and try it out thoroughly beforehand, e. g. on a patient lion at the zoo or on the swans in a city park.

From the point of view of photographic technique, there are three things which should be particularly borne in mind when using these long zoom lenses.

Firstly, these big calibres only open their eyes at fairly high exposure values – either you need a

great deal of light to use them or you have to fall back on highly sensitive films (Ektachrome 400, for instance).

Secondly, every movement the photographer makes is magnified out of all proportion. To overcome the risk of wobble, which is particularly great with these lenses, you should either use short exposure times of at least 1/250 sec., or, even better, 1/500 sec., or carry a tripod round with you. For greater mobility and speed, I prefer to work freehand. The film I like best is Kodachrome 64, which I expose in the clear morning or afternoon sun, depending on how bright my subject appears, at aperture 8 and a shutter speed of 1/250 sec., or even 1/500 sec.

Thirdly these giant lenses only give sharp photos if you set the distance exactly. The only photographers to take home razor-sharp bird or gazelle portraits are those who take the trouble to adjust the distance ever so slightly until the sharpest point on their subject has been found. And it is exactly for this precision that there is usually so little time, because the "model" seldom adopts a certain pose long enough for the photographer to adjust his camera down to the last millimetre.

Photographic masterpieces are therefore rather the exception than the rule. However, don't let this discourage you – every animal photographer has to live with it! It is at all events fun to go hunting with a camera.

By the way, make sure to take enough film with you. Although most of the bigger lodges stock all the common types of film, the prices are so high as to take all the joy out of photography.

# Kilaguni

It was late afternoon when we reached Kilaguni Lodge, situated in the western part of Tsavo Park. The marabou-storks had already taken up their sleeping places on a huge baobab tree which spread its branches a few hundred yards from the steel gate to this tourist caravanserai.

After I had stowed away my things in the comfortably equipped room (every unit has a bathtub and a toilet – and that in the middle of the bush), I took a long dip in the pleasantly cool swimming pool to forget the heat of the Land Rover trip.

Later, I met my travel companions near the well-stocked bar, where they had already occupied the best seats for the evening show. Somebody gave me a sundowner – one of those drinks in tropical countries to console yourself with at sunset.

I had just enough time to try out my whisky before the performance started. A chain of elephants came trotting. The thirsty animals hurried the last few yards to the water hole, their trunks swinging round their front legs like loose ships' hawsers. A few seconds later these animal giants stood side by side at the water's edge and sucked the delicious liquid bucket-wise into their trunks and then squirted it into their throats.

From between the pillar-like legs a small baby elephant gingerly approached the water. It hadn't yet learned how to use its trunk like a hose pipe, and had to bend its heavy head laboriously down to the surface of the water. At its third attempt it lost its balance, of course, and landed head over heels with a big splash. A splutter of subdued laughter from the gallery (nobody wanted

to scare the animals away with too much merriment) accompanied the evening's first climax.

The watering place, artificially created with the construction of the lodge, guarantees an entertainment programme with a great deal of variety. This luxury lodge situated in the middle of a picturesque volcanic landscape – the tip of a mighty lava stream stops only a few hundred yards from the door – enables the traveller to experience Africa and its animal kingdom in the original state without the usual creature comforts.

The buffaloes came between the prawn cocktail and the T-bone steak – about 120 of them, huge black figures whose eyes sparkled in the floodlights like reflectors. The animals in the vicinity have long grown accustomed to the bright lights which turn the watering-hole, night after night, into a unique circus ring, in which they give fascinating performances at their own will. The noise of the buffaloes stamping through the mud together with their deep rumbles made for a most unusual musical accompaniment to our meal.

The view of the water hole is completely open – there are no windows or support constructions in the way. During the dessert the guests raised not only their spoons, but suddenly also their binoculars – a striped hyena was snuffling noisily around near the herd. A shy loner, the hyena is seldom seen during daylight hours.

During coffee, which, according to a good old English custom, rounds off the dinner, talk inevitably turned to safari experiences. The neighbours on our right had been able to watch a group of three cheetahs out on the hunt, whereas two Swiss tourists on our left had discovered a rhinoceros. They had really been in luck, because, compared with earlier times, when a few thousands rhinos inhabited Tsavo Park, there are today less than a hundred who hide in this, the biggest of Kenya's national parks.

A few drinks later – the herd of buffaloes had long since disappeared, and most of the spectators had already gone off to bed – a whisper suddenly went through the small group of remaining guests: two yellow figures emerged from the darkness and trotted lazily down to the water's edge. Lions! It had been worth while waiting. The regular slurping of the predators' drinking was easy to hear through the still of the night. Nobody spoke. The presence of the lions had the same effect on us as on our forefathers, who would huddle closer to the fire when they felt threatened by the sudden appearance of these mighty cats.

Just as quietly as they came the two night prowlers loped away again. Complete silence descended for a while – even the clinking of whisky glasses finally stopped.

Some time in the night I was wakened by gurgling noises. From my bed I could make out three huge bull elephants which were drinking their fill at the watering-hole with all the time in the world.

In the morning the warbling of a bird choir woke me from my sleep. The first baboons noisily left the tree in which they had slept – only about 50 yards away. As I was enjoying a few sips of my early morning coffee which a friendly steward had brought to my bedside, two weighty pashas were fighting for the favours of a particulary pretty she-ape. On my way to the swimming pool, early morning work out, etc., the sight of snow-bedecked Mt. Kilimanjaro, rising majestically above the morning mist, made me catch my first deep breath.

We were still breakfasting when the zebras came. Their black and white stripes were mirrored in the water. Impalas joined them – and were suddenly scared by a troop of wart hogs hurrying to the water hole, tails sticking up in the air. A few oryx antelopes hesitantly approached down a beaten runway; however, once at the water's edge they energetically made room for themselves with their long horns.

In the thornbushes which spread out only a few yards away from the balcony wall, hornbills and glossy starlings performed gymnastic feats and occasionally picked up crumbs of toast and other titbits on bold excursions to the tables in the dining room.

Suddenly two grey hands appeared at the top of the wall, to be followed by a hairy face – like a Kilroy drawing, a young baboon popped up and eyed the breakfast plates of the surprised guests! Before a serviette-brandishing waiter could shoo him away, he had clambered over the stone barricade and, on a lightning-quick sally, captured a silver milk-jug which he took with him as he beat a hasty retreat and then licked empty to the grins of the spectators.

According to our itinerary we were to leave after breakfast for our next goal. A pity – we would dearly have liked to see a few more performances in Kilaguni on this marvellous open-air stage.

# Kenya's Coast

The boat pitched sluggishly between the waves. I leaned against the mast, let the sun dry my skin and enjoyed the soporific up-and-down. A few hundred yards away a stony monster rose from the water, a coral reef which from a distance was reminiscent of the shape of a turtle. This has given the bay its name: Turtle Bay.

About half a mile from the sandy beach the breakers drew a white line through the deep blue water of the Indian Ocean. This marks the position of the reef, which is located off the greater part of the Kenyan coast and which protects the shallow water zones in front of the beaches against sharks.

The roar of the surf and the whistling of the passat wind were irresistibly seductive, and I enjoyed daydreaming while listening to them. In the morning I had dived down between the coral colonies to watch the zebrafish and parrotfish, had observed an octopus continuously changing colour and finally had visited a lobster in its rocky grotto.

These coral gardens hidden only a few feet below the surface offered, in such a confined space, such a profusion of mysterious living forms and colours that the images from this underwater walk swam before my eyes for the rest of the day.

To protect the unique marine life in this bay, the Kenyan government has declared the area a national park – one in which you don't go on safari so much as snorkel or dive.

After an extensive evening stroll along a blindingly white sandy beach I travelled back to Malindi, a charming little town on the Indian Ocean coast which had made Vasco da Gama and his fleet welcome and which today, as one of the magnets of Kenyan tourism, exerts a considerable pull on holidaymakers from all over the world.

Between the houses of the town and the sea, a broad sandy beach stretches for miles and is never too full, even during the high season from December to March. This beach invites you to go for walks, the length of which is only determined by the sundial of your own shadow.

The water is warm, 28 °C (82 °F), and the waves caress bathers like sea nymphs. And in the evenings, it's off to the disco. The hotels are anxious to entertain their guests with a varied programme – barbecues, folklore shows, film shows, discos or simply soft music accompanying the rustling of the palm trees. Even lovers of hot and very hot nightlife can get what they want in the various bars and night-clubs, although they may sometimes have to pay a lot for it!

Malindi's out-and-out tropical climate at first makes you just want to bathe and idle the time away. However, from here you can take part in safaris and excursions of all kinds and to all parts of Kenya. Malindi has its own airport, to which there are daily scheduled flights by Kenya

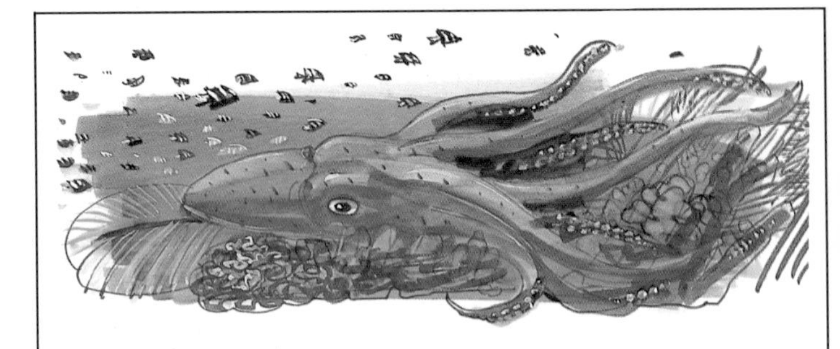

Airways, and from which air safaris to the various national parks and other destinations start.

As in Malindi, beach hotels are spreading out to the north and south of the port of Mombasa. The modern harbour of this old seafarers' town supplies not only Kenya with oil and commercial goods, but also a number of neighbouring countries. Consequently, the streets, stores and bars of Mombasa are as busy as you would expect them to be, and the music is just as loud and varied as the life in the bars and pubs round the harbour. After shopping or strolling around the town it is pleasant to flee from the heat of the day and take refuge on the balcony of Castle Hotel, drink a cool beer and listen to the laughter of the sailors and their beautiful girlfriends for the day, or just to watch the passers-by.

Kenya's coast is as if a bit of the South Seas had been transplanted to East Africa – mile after mile of empty beaches, palm groves, coral colonies, outriggers which the fishermen go fishing in, people with their happy attitude to life – "pole, pole" (slow, slow): don't rush when it's hot! The coast is also the breakers, pounding day and night against the reef, the gentle breeze caressing the skin, the small villages spreading out in the shade of the coconut-trees – and a lot more besides.

The coast also includes Lamu, a small island town in the north, which has changed but little down the centuries and on which there are, apart from one government car, no motorised vehicles. What Lamu does have, though, is narrow alleyways and small Arabian restaurants to tempt the hungry tourist.

In the evening the natives, many of them in their flowing white robes, go for a stroll down the alleys, drink tea with their friends, or gather round some board game. The marvellously carved door-frames which can be found in some house entrances are famous. Lamu – an exotic little town in whose corners and under whose arches the fairy-tale world of the Arabian Nights seems to live on like a mirage.

*Künkel*

# History of Kenya

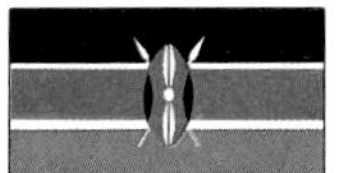

The history of East Africa is particularly interesting because the origins of mankind are now thought to lie in the African continent. While many believed for years that Asia would prove to be the birthplace of man, important archaeological finds in South and East Africa suggest that the ancestors of modern man emerged here as many as 2.5 million years ago (i. e. during the Tertiary period of geological development).

The first skull belonging to this earliest identified ancestor of man (Australopithecus africanus) was found in Taungs, South Africa in 1924 by Raymond Dart. At around the same time the famous anthropologists Dr. Louis Leakey and Dr. Mary Leakey were working in the Great Rift Valley in East Africa. There they found fossil skulls of protohumans, the best-known probably being that of Zinjanthropus found in the Olduvai Gorge in northwest Tanzania. In addition, the Leakeys were able to identify bipedal footprints in cemented mud. These footprints, proven to be those of the hominid, were evidence of his already having made the transition from four to two legs.

The most advanced of the early East African hominids was Homo habilis, so named by Leakey because of its ability to shape and use primitive stone tools.

In 1972 the Leakey's son, Richard Leakey, found a fossil skull with a large cranial capacity east of Lake Turkana (Lake Rudolf up to 1975) in north Kenya. The skull was estimated to be 2.6 million years old. This find remains unique but evidence of stones having been shaped into tools, as well as skeletal remains of other humanoids led Leakey to surmise that Homo habilis had also been in the area at that time.

Evidence then of early man having left arboreal dwellings, where climbing necessitated the use of all four limbs, for more open country. There has been much speculation about why this move took place but it is clear that once on open terrain and involved in hunting (the development of primitive stone tools meant that meat became part of his diet) proto-man would need to rise up on his hind legs more and more often and would eventually come to walk upright. Surveillance of the surrounding area, self-defence, hunting and the carrying of food would thus be facilitated, and early man emerged as a hunter and gatherer in the savanna regions.

At a time roughly corresponding with the emergence of modern man (i. e. approx. 100,000 years ago) stone tools became more refined and efficient, enabling man to enter forest regions in search of food, and to fish. Later came the important development of the bow and arrow which greatly increased his efficiency as a hunter.

In the course of time, however, the hunters and gatherers lost the most fertile areas of the savanna to agriculturalists who had developed the use of iron tools. Pastoralism and the cultivation of crops had developed over many hundreds of years and it is thought that cattle had been kept in the highlands of East Africa as long ago as 1000 B. C. Iron mining and forging marked a significant breakthrough in agricultural techniques.

Up to now we have really been discussing the history of mankind in Africa. The arrival of Arab merchants and the foundation of an Arab trading post on the Indian Ocean, Mombasa, were important events in the more recent history of the coast. The Arab influence along the coast from the 7th to the 13th centuries was substantial and is still evident today. But this is not to say that the area lost its identity to Islam.

Improved agricultural methods, the keeping of livestock and the development of crafts had meant that trading had begun between different African groups before the arrival of the Arabs. The latter made the area into a thriving centre of trade with settlements in Lamu, Kalifi, Malindi, Pemba Island and the legendary Zanzibar, but the coast remained African in essence, the people of the city-states being mainly Swahili.

In 1498 the Portuguese explorer, Vasco da Gama rounded the Cape of Good Hope, sailed up the East African coast and landed in Malindi.

With the arrival of the Portuguese the struggle began for control of Mombasa and the trade routes along the coast. It was a struggle which was to last for around 200 years, and in the course of which Mombasa was to change hands repeatedly. 1593 saw the completion of the Portuguese Fort Jesus. This castle was thought to be impregnable, but throughout the many years of conflict the Swahili city-states (with the support of Omani Arabs) resisted all Portuguese attempts to control the area, and were eventually victorious. In 1698, after a three-year siege of Fort Jesus, the Portuguese lost Mombasa to the Sultan of Muscat and Oman. It wasn't, however, until 1728 that the Portuguese were finally ousted by the Arabs.

The Arabs too were ambitious to control trade routes along the East African coast and this led to conflicts with many of the Swahili cities. In 1828 the whole coast (encompassing present-day Kenya, Tanzania and Somalia) became the independent Sultanate of Zanzibar. In 1840 Sayyid Said, a ruler of Muscat, made Zanzibar his new capital, a move which brought more stability to the area and meant that all, including the Swahili cities, enjoyed a certain amount of prosperity.

The U. S., British and French governments established consulates in the Sultanate during the first half of the nineteenth century.

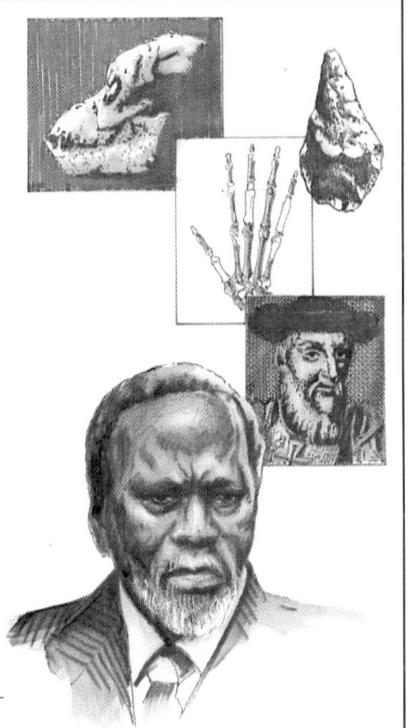

*Bones and tool finds of early man; the Portuguese explorer, Vasco da Gama; Kenya's first president, Jomo Kenyatta . . . representatives of important stages in Kenya's long history.*

After the abolition of slavery in British Territories in 1807, pressure was brought to bear on the Imam Sayyid Said, and he eventually agreed to a treaty prohibiting the sale of slaves to Christian countries. It was not, however, until 1873 that the slave market in Zanzibar was closed, and even then black market trading continued. Emancipation of the last remaining slaves in the area did not take place until 1907.

Interest among the British people in the slavery issue (colonialist tendencies would emerge later) meant that the nineteenth century saw the arrival of many missionaries and explorers in Africa. In 1844 the Church Missionary Society sent Ludwig Krapf to East Africa, where he established a missionary station outside Mombasa. Two years later he was joined by Johann Rebmann. In 1849 Krapf and Rebman became the first whites to penetrate the interior. (The first white settlers would not arrive until 1902.) Other well-known missionaries and pioneers were Dr. David Livingstone, who worked for years as a missionary and discovered the Victoria Falls in 1855, and Burton and Speke, who on a joint expedition in 1858 discovered Lake Tanganyika.

Towards the end of the 19th century the "scramble for Africa" began. The balance of power in Europe was such that the major nations sought to establish "spheres of influence" overseas. Africa was seen as ideal territory because of the opportunities for trade it represented, and numerous protective treaties with native leaders were sealed.

In 1884 Dr. Karl Peters established the Society for German Colonization and concluded protection treaties with the chiefs of Usagara, Useguha, Ukami and Nguru. These treaties were tantamount to colonization and were recognized as such by the German emperor, Wilhelm, and his chancellor, Bismarck, in 1885. In the same year the territory was extended to include present-day Tanzania and became German East Africa, a protectorate of the German Empire.

The course of events leading to the acquisition of territory for Britain was similar. In 1887 the area between the Umba River and Kipini (part of present-day Kenya) passed from the Sultan of Zanzibar into the hands of the British East Africa Association (which later became the Imperial British East Africa Company).

In 1890 Britain and Germany concluded the Zanzibar Treaty. Pemba Island and Zanzibar were made a British protectorate, Heligoland became German.

The Imperial British East Africa Company, wishing to open up East Africa to greater trade by building a railway linking Mombasa on the Indian Ocean with Uganda, approached the British government for financial backing. To protect its investments the British government declared Uganda a temporary British protectorate, a move which eventually led to the acquisition of more territory. In time the Sultan of Zanzibar's coastal strip and all of present-day Kenya became the East Africa Protectorate. With the establishment of the latter the stage was set for colonial rule of Kenya and Uganda – a state of affairs which was to last some 70 years.

1896 was an important year in Kenya's history as construction began on the railway between Mombasa and Uganda. It would take until 1901 for construction work to reach Kilindi on Lake Victoria, the final stretch to Kampala being completed some thirty years later.

With a view to gaining some returns on its investment in railway construction, and having recognized the agricultural potential of the area, the British government encouraged white settlement in Nairobi (established as construction headquarters in 1899) and in the surrounding highlands.

It is interesting to note that this was the area traditionally inhabited by the Kikuyu people. The Kikuyu would therefore be the first Kenyans to experience the loss of homelands to whites. On the other hand it would be the Kikuyu who would benefit first and foremost from the educational advantages afforded by white settlement in Kenya. For although serious mistakes were certainly made and the enlightened views of the Foreign Office not implemented wholeheartedly, the colonial masters did do a great deal in establishing seminaries and eventually schools and colleges. Higher educational standards ultimately led to greater political awareness and to hopes among the Kenyan people that they would one day gain their independence. The Kikuyu became a kind of Kenyan elite, led the Mau Mau movement in the 1950s and were therefore instrumental in gaining Kenyan independence.

The First World War saw British and German troops fighting outside Dar es Salaam, the capital of German East Africa. Those with a particular interest in military history will probably remember names like those of Jan Christiaan Smuts and Paul von Lettow-Vorbeck. After fighting for the Boers in the Boer War, Smuts joined the Allies in both World Wars and it was he who reversed the first German victories and in fact took most of Tanganyika. As for the German, von Lettow-Vorbeck, whilst most of the German forces surrended in the face of Allied superiority, his troops held out until Armistice.

After the First World War German colonies were divided and Tanganyika became part of British East Africa. The end of the war saw no fundamental change in the attitude of the vast majority of the African people towards colonialism and their own subordinate position within the system. It is clear, however, that educated Africans had by this time moved too far away from their tribal traditions ever to return to them again, and that this would inevitably mean change. Kenya had its own stock of intellectuals but their participation in government was rejected by the colonial masters.

In 1920 Kenya became a British Crown Colony, the coastal strip retaining its status of a protectorate under the sovereignty of the Sultan of Zanzibar. The colony was administered by a governor who was ultimately responsible to the British crown; Africans were only involved in the lower levels of judicial administration.

Capital investment in the colony brought improvements in the living standards of the white settlers but there was no effective change in the day to day lives of the black Kenyans. The latter felt the indignity of seeing their traditional homelands in the hands of a foreign power, and suffered as a result of heavy taxation. Both led in time to unrest and even organized opposition. It was, for example, in the 1920s that the Pan-Africa Movement began in the U. S. A. At the same time Jomo Kenyatta was in England on behalf of the Kikuyu Central Association presenting Kenya's case to the Foreign Office. (When he finally returned to Kenya in 1947 Kenyatta became president of the Kenya African Union.) The protests of the Kikuyu (their grievances would be the main driving force behind Mau Mau) had begun as early as 1921 when the Young Kikuyu Association was formed, and its leader, Harry Thuku, called on the people to react against the heavy hut tax they were paying to the British.

The establishment of independent African churches also marked a breaking of ties with Europe. Changes in attitude and the establishment of autonomous African organizations would accelerate as a result of the Second World War.

In the Second World War Kenya was again a theatre of war, this time

# Mau Mau

If any one particular episode of Kenyan history is familiar to people all around the world, it is surely the Mau Mau rebellion of the 1950s.

Mau Mau came about as a direct result of 70 years of colonial rule in Kenya and was indicative of a total lack of understanding of the African people on the part of the colonial rulers.

Those who first encouraged white settlement in the fertile highlands of Kenya gave no consideration to the rights or wishes of the native population. When, years later, opposition to colonial rule began to develop into an organized and publicized movement (first of all in the 1920s but more especially after the Second World War), the colonial masters saw this as the work of a few militants. Seeking to protect their own interests and "their" land, they set out to quash any revolutionary tendencies by interning leading figures and declaring all opposition to the colonial system to be illegal. They certainly did not believe that the fight would continue without leadership – but then they failed to understand that the people were not interested in any vague political principles but were fighting for their land and their freedom.

The end of the Second World War saw the emergence of African politics and marked a turning point in African history. In Kenya the Kenya African Union was formed; Jomo Kenyatta, back home after years of campaigning for Kenyan independence in England, became its president. For the first time in their history the interests of all the Kenyan people were represented under one banner, and the struggle for independence really began.

Campaigning was peaceful at first but when only token changes in policy were made some protesters lost patience and resorted to more violent means. No deaths occurred, however, until 1952 when the situation was deemed to be out of hand and the government declared a state of emergency. It was in response to this that the Mau Mau rebellion took place. Thousands of Kenyans, mainly Kikuyus, took to the hills around Nairobi. There guerrillas organized campaigns aimed at driving white settlers out of Kenya, and civilians sought refuge from the 50,000 British troops brought in to deal with the situation. Measures taken by the British government were severe and more than 10,000 Kenyans lost their lives. A further 90,000 were imprisoned in concentration camps, and many many more were driven from their homes and forced to live in specially designated villages so as to prevent their supporting the guerrillas. British losses in comparison were minimal. 100 people were killed (the figure includes members of the security forces).

Mau Mau was unique in the African Nationalist Movement as a whole because he Kenyan people fought in effect without leaders, the latter having been placed under arrest by the colonial powers at the first sign of trouble. Jomo Kenyatta and other leading figures in the Kenya African Union were convicted of having organized the revolt and were imprisoned in 1953. Their involvement in the violence was never, however, and it now seems unlikely that they had any active part in it. They would, of course, have welcomed and benefit from the pressure it brought to bear on the British government.

This was the real victory of Mau Mau. Because although the guerrillas were defeated in 1956 by the superior forces of the British army, they had by then made it quite clear to the Foreign Office at Westminster that there was no future for the colonial system. Seven years later Kenya became an independent nation and the new president, Kenyatta, could proclaim the slogan for the new Kenya: HARAMBEE – "Let us come together and work together".

for Allied campaigns against Italian Somaliland and Ethiopia.

Of greater significance, however, was the fact that Africa spent the war years providing the Allies with materials needed for military campaigns. Increased production in mines and on plantations led to the demise of rural communities as more and more people headed for the towns in the hope of better conditions there.

The growth of production industries in the West after the war meant that raw materials were still very much in demand and that, in order to satisfy this demand, the migration of people from rural communities to what were rapidly becoming urban slums continued.

It was soon clear that the whole structure of African society as established during the years of colonial rule was disintegrating and that there was no solution within the framework of colonialism. Meeting in 1945, the sixth Pan-African Congress (Jomo Kenyatta was a member of the Congress) spoke of the need for autonomy and even independence.

Though Britain had emerged from the war impoverished, there was a mood of tolerance in the country and the Labour government was aware of the need for change in the policy in Africa. Declaring British colonies sovereign members of the Commonwealth of Nations was a convenient way of responding to demands for change but could never be satisfactory. The fight for "Uhuru" (freedom, autonomy and independence) continued and in 1952 the Mau Mau campaigns of the Kikuyu began. (See inset.)

Incidentally, it was also in 1952 that Princess Elizabeth, holidaying in the now famous Treetops Hotel, learned of the death of her father, King George VI. She paid an official visit to Kenya in 1983, her first since becoming English monarch.

In the Lancaster House Conference of 1960 Britain finally agreed to majority rule in Kenya. It was not, however, until December 12th 1963 that the Kenyan people gained full independence.

Jomo Kenyatta had been president of the Kenya African National Union (KANU) since 1961, and in 1963 he became the first president of Independent Kenya, a position he held until his death in 1978.

During the 1960s a great many African nations would gain their independence, a "wind of change" sweeping the whole continent. But this period of change was not without its problems. Africans took over senior positions in government and administration but the institutions which they directed had always been, and were still, based on European models. There were two possible courses of action – the creation of a black elite to take over where the colonial rulers had left off, or the dismantling of all social and political structures. Neither alternative assured a peaceful period of transition. Additional difficulties included the not inconsiderable influence of traditional cultures, the problems inherent in the rapid growth of the urban slums and the question of how to unite the population itself. Due to the fact that formal education was not widespread at this time, the people of Kenya had become divided into an illiterate majority and what can only be described as an educated elite.

The fact that Kenya was a one-party state also created problems as the formation of opposition parties tended to take the form of conspiracies against the government. There were, for example, incidents involving leaders of the Luo (a Nilotic people living east of Lake Victoria) which were indicative of the prevalent anti-Luo feeling in the land at this time. Retaining law and order was at times no easy task for President Kenyatta.

One of the most important reforms after independence was the division of 3 million hectares of agricultural land which had, until 1960, been in the hands of white settlers. The "Million Acre Settlement Scheme" redistributed this land among 34,000 Kenyan families, the British Government undertaking to pay compensation to

# History at a Glance

| | |
|---|---|
| **2.5 million years ago (Tertiary Period)** | Protohumans present in East Africa. |
| **100,000 years ago** | Hunters and gatherers roam the area. |
| **1st–5th centuries A. D.** | Tribes begin to use metal implements. Bantu-speaking peoples cultivate crops. |
| **7th–13th centuries** | Coast under Arab influence. |
| **1498** | Portuguese explorer Vasco da Gama lands at Malindi. Start of 200-year struggle for control of the coastal area and trade routes. |
| **1593** | Completion of the "impregnable" Portuguese Fort Jesus. Mombasa thought to be safe from further Arab attack. |
| **1696–98** | Siege of Fort Jesus. Mombasa lost to the Sultan of Muscat and Oman. |
| **1828** | Coast becomes the independent Sultanate of Zanzibar. |
| **1840** | Sayyid Said transfers his capital to Zanzibar. |
| **1836, 1840, 1844** | Establishment of U. S., British and French consulates in Zanzibar. |
| **1873** | The slave market is closesd in Zanzibar after more than 50 years of campaigning on the part of enlightened nations. |
| **19th century** | Many missionaries and explorers venture into Africa. |
| **Late 19th century** | The "scramble for Africa" begins with European nations negotiating "treaties of protection" with natives in order to gain influence in trade, etc. |
| **1884** | Dr. Karl Peters establishes the Society for German Colonization. |
| **1885** | German East Africa comes into being. |
| **1887** | Part of present-day Kenya passes to the Imperial British East Africa Company courtesy of the Sultan of Zanzibar. |

| | |
|---|---|
| **1890** | Zanzibar Treaty. Pemba Island and Zanzibar are made a British Protectorate. In return Heligoland passes from the British to the Germans. |
| **1896** | Construction work begins on the railway between Mombasa and Uganda. White settlement encouraged by the British Government. |
| **1902** | First white settlers arrive in Nairobi and establish plantations in the fertile highlands. Establishment of seminaries and later of schools and colleges. Those to benefit in the first instance are members of the Kikuyu people, in whose traditional homelands the whites settle. The Kikuyu will later be the driving force behind Mau Mau. |
| **1919** | After the First World War territories constituting German East Africa are divided. Tanganyika becomes part of British East Africa. Kenya now has its own stock of intellectuals but their participation in political processes is rejected. |
| **1920** | Kenya becomes a British Crown Colony. Blacks involved only in lower levels of judicial administration. |
| **1920s and 30s** | Pan-Africa Movement has its origins in the U. S. A. Jomo Kenyatta is abroad and begins publicising the case for Kenyan independence. |
| **1948** | The end of the Second World War sees ever greater self-awareness among black Africans. Development of African National Movements. British colonies become sovereign members of the Commonwealth but there are no fundamental changes in government or administration. |
| **1952** | Mau Mau. Britain declares a state of emergency in Kenya, there are mass arrests and many Kenyans lose their lives in the struggle for independence. |
| **1960** | Lancaster House Conference. Britain finally agrees to majority rule for Kenya. |
| **1961** | Jomo Kenyatta becomes president of the Kenya African National Union. |
| **1963** | Kenya gains independence, Kenyatta becomes president, a position he holds until his death in 1978. |

| | |
|---|---|
| **1967** | Daniel arap Moi is appointed vice-president of Kenya. Kenya, Tanzania and Uganda form the East African Community. |
| **1976** | Entebbe hostage incident. |
| **1977** | East African Community is dissolved. Tanzania closes border with Kenya. |
| **1978** | Death of Jomo Kenyatta. |
| **1983** | Renewed attempts to re-unite Kenya and Tanzania. |
| | Border between Kenya and Tanzania re-opened. |

dispossessed whites. The plan was completed in 1979.

In 1967 Daniel arap Moi was appointed vice-president, a position he held until he became president after the death of President Kenyatta in 1978.

In 1967 Kenya, Tanzania and Uganda united to form the East African Community, the aim of which was to promote social and economic ties between the member states.

In 1971 Idi Amin became head of state in neighbouring Uganda. Relations between Kenya and Uganda deteriorated considerably when Amin claimed part of West Kenya for Uganda. The hostage affair at Entebbe Airport, when Israelis intervened successfully using Kenya as their base, made matters very tense.

In 1977 the East African Community was dissolved. In February of the same year Tanzania closed its border with Kenya after disagreement between President Nyerere of Tanzania and President Kenyatta.

In August 1978 an aged President Kenyatta died. He has remained one of the most important figures in modern Africa. Daniel arap Moi became president. He carried on as Kenyatta would have wanted him to. Important reforms were put (at least officially) into effect. There was, for example, legislation making circumcision of girls illegal. However, the country also had to implement drastic economic measures including cutbacks in health and education programmes.

In 1983 Presidents Moi and Nyerere met (together with President Obote of Uganda) to renew attempts to unite the countries. In the same year Tanzania reopened its border with Kenya.

In spite of difficulties and periods of unrest Kenya has remained a relatively stable and prosperous nation. The very large tourist industry is of particular value in the economy.

# Location and Landscape

Nairobi is 4,239 miles from London by air; in eight hours non-stop another world is reached. For those crossing the Atlantic the journey is somewhat longer and more arduous, but within twenty hours and after just three stops they too will arrive in Kenya's capital.

The term "East Africa" is generally taken to mean that area of eastern Africa extending over the equator and comprising the countries Kenya, Tanzania and Uganda.

Kenya is bounded by Ethiopia and the Sudan in the north, by Somalia in the east, by Uganda in the west, and by Tanzania in the south. The Kenya-Tanzania border is an almost straight line running northwest to southeast with one bend around Mt. Kilimanjaro (in Tanzania). In the southeast the Indian Ocean forms the coastline.

Kenya covers an area of 582,646 sq. km (224,960 sq. miles). Most of its approximately 18 million inhabitants live in an area between Mombasa on the coast, Lake Victoria in the southwest corner, and Lake Turkana in the north.

**Nairobi,** the Kenyan capital, is not central but enjoys a climatically favourable position at 1,650 m (5,500 ft) above sea level. It is situated on the Ngara Nairobi River and at the foot of the 5,199 m (17,058 ft) high Mt. Kenya. Although directly on the equator, the high altitude of Mt. Kenya (it is higher than any of the peaks of the Rockies) has allowed for the formation of glaciers and an ice cap.

The plateau on which Nairobi stands and the surrounding highlands constitute the **fertile interior** of Kenya – an area which extends to the shores of Lake Victoria in the west. A fairly narrow **coastal strip** is also suitable for intensive agriculture (in particular the cultivation of rice and coconuts); otherwise only subsistence farming is possible. This accounts for the low population density in other areas.

**Lake Victoria,** the world's second largest freshwater lake after Lake Superior in North America, has an area of 69,485 sq. km (26,828 sq. miles). It lies in Kenya, Tanzania and Uganda, and is the main source of the Nile (the headstream of the Nile, the Luvironza, rises in Burundi, flows into Lake Victoria, and leaves it as the Victoria Nile). From Kenya, the Mara, Nzoia and Yala rivers flow into the lake. Lake Victoria lies at an altitude of 1,134 m (3,720 ft), in a shallow depression on otherwise elevated ground between the two troughs of the Great Rift Valley.

The **Great Rift Valley,** a phenomena resulting from movements in the earth's crust during geological evolution, when tension exerted by parallel faults caused the land to subside, is one of the longest rift systems in the world. It extends from the Red Sea through Ethiopia, Kenya and Tanzania (it bifurcates in East Africa) into southern Africa.

In some parts of Kenya the Rift Valley is an impressive 50 km (31 miles) wide, and in the central highlands it can be as deep as 3,000 m (over 9,000 ft). Its presence in Kenya is further emphasised by the lakes which lie along it like pearls on a string.

**Lake Turkana** (Lake Rudolf until 1975) is 7,104 sq. km (2,743 sq. miles) in area, and is the largest of Kenya's lakes. Long and narrow, it lies in the north of the country, at the border with Ethiopia but almost entirely in Kenya.

Lying almost equidistant from Turkana and Victoria but still in the eastern through of the Rift Valley is **Lake Baringo.** Nineteen km (12 miles) in length, Baringo is tiny in comparison with either of the huge lakes, Turkana or Victoria. There are a number of islets on the lake, one of which has hot (sulphurous) springs.

Moving in a southerly direction, **Lake Bogoria** or Hannington (with hot springs and a geysir on its western shore) follows; then comes **Lake Nakuru,** another salt water lake, only 2.7 m (9 ft) deep; and southeast of Nakuru there is **Lake Elmenteita,** a soda lake which reaches a depth of only 1.9 m (6 ft). **Lake Naivasha,** a freshwater lake and the highest of the Rift lakes, lies northwest of Nairobi. South of the capital lies **Lake Magadi,** the world's most abundant source of soda ash. Magadi's soda deposits are continually and naturally renewed although they have been exploited since the beginning of the century. The almost adjacent Lake Natron (also a soda lake as its name implies) is on Tanzanian territory. Its soda yield is, however, not as high as that of Magadi.

Hot springs and seeping magma (as experienced at Lake Bogoria) are evidence of **volcanic activity** in the Rift Valley. Kilimanjaro in Tanzania, Mt. Kenya and Mt. Meru in Kenya, and Mt. Elgon in Uganda are all extinct volcanoes. (The huge

# Kenya: Facts and Figures

**Location:** Kenya is part of East Africa and covers an area of 582,646 sq. km (224,960 sq. miles). It borders on Somalia in the east, on Ethiopia and the Sudan in the north, on Uganda in the west, and on Tanzania in the south. The Indian Ocean forms Kenya's southeast boundary. The equator runs virtually through the centre of Kenya.

**Form of Government:** Kenya is an independent republic. The Kenyan people gained their independence on 12th December 1963. There is only one political party in Kenya – the Kenya African National Union (KANU). The leader of KANU, Daniel arap Moi is also president (Jomo Kenyatta's successor, he has held the position since 1978). The system of government is democratic. The president is elected for a five year term; his cabinet is responsible to parliament, which consists of a single chamber, called the National Assembly. 158 members of parliament are elected, 12 are appointed by the president. Elections take place every five years. The constitution dates from 1969 and assures freedom of speech, assembly and worship.

**Population:** According to a 1982 estimate, Kenya has a population of 18,200,000 (in 1979 the figure was 15,322,000). Population growth is currently 4%, one of the highest rates in the world. Population density is 31.2 inhabitants per square kilometre. In densely populated areas, i. e. in the highlands, along the coast and around Lake Victoria, population density can be as much as 200 inhabitants per square kilometre.

The Kenyan population is made up of four main ethnic groups: Bantu, Nilotic, Hamitic and Nilo-Hamitic peoples. More than 60% of the people belong to the Bantu group (20% Kikuyu, 13% Abaluhya, 11% Kamba); Nilotic, Hamitic and Nilo-Hamitic groups make up approximately 30% (the Luo are a Nilotic tribe, the tall Somali nomads of northeast Kenya are a Hamitic group, the Masai belong to the Nilo-Hamites). A further 80,000 Asians, 27,000 Arabs and 25,000 Europeans also live in Kenya.

**Language:** Official languages are Swahili and English.

**Religion:** Approximately 30% of the population are Protestants, 22% are Catholics, and 5% are Muslims. Many religious sects also exist, above all, around Lake Victoria. Animism continues to be an important element in the spiritual lives of many Kenyans.

Ngorongoro crater in Tanzania is a special phenomena – a volcanic explosion has left the crater considerably enlarged, forming a caldera.)

Many **rivers** and streams flow through the area between the highlands and the coast. Of these, the Tana, the longest river in Kenya, rises in the Aberdare Ranges, flows eastwards in a wide bow, and enters the Indian Ocean at Kipini (just south of Lamu Island). The Athi rises in the southeast highlands and flows into the Galana in the Tsavo National Park; the Galana then flows on towards Malindi and the Indian Ocean. In addition, the Ewaso Ng'iro rises in the Aberdares, flows along the northern edge of the highlands and then into the Lorian Swamp of northeast Kenya.

A large sedimentary delta has formed where the Tana enters the ocean. Where there are no deltas or bays long stretches of **fine sand beaches** characterize the Kenyan coastline. The whole of the East African coast is shielded from the full force of the ocean swell by **coral reefs** – an underwater paradise not far from idyllic beaches.

There are coral islands off almost every section of the coast. The most important of these islands are (from north to south) Pate Island, Lamu Island and Mombasa – yes, the latter occupies the whole island, and much more!

Dense **mangrove swamps** are also to be found along parts of the coast. Extensive felling of the mangrove forests for timber export to the Arab world has meant that the natural balance of these areas has been destroyed – in some places to an alarming degree.

Between the coast and the fertile highlands are the dry grass plains and thorn bushes of the **savanna.** Most of Kenya's national parks are to be found in this area. (See chapter "National Parks".)

Moving northwards from the densely populated highlands towards Lake Turkana, the fertile landscape gives way to one of **sand and volcanic rubble.** This region is only sparsely populated; the scene is one of desolation. Rocks and eroded volcanoes give way in turn to the deserts of the Ethiopian border and beyond.

# Climate

The most important factor determining climatic conditions in Kenya is altitude. For, although Kenya lies on the equator, approximately half the country (including Nairobi and most of the national parks) is more than 1,500 m above sea level and therefore enjoys a **temperate climate.**

In the highlands sunshine is plentiful but altitude makes for fresher conditions than we might expect – humidity levels are low. Temperatures are fairly constant all year – an average 24 °C (75 °F) – dropping, however, to an average 11 °C (52 °F) at night. This means that warm clothing is absolutely essential for cool evenings in Nairobi. The same applies to evenings in the bush – although days will have been characterized by dust and heat, those on safari will be glad of a warm pullover after sunset.

Rainfall is also plentiful in the highlands, especially around Lake Victoria and on higher slopes.

There are two rainy seasons in Kenya. The long rains last from the end of March to the beginning of June; the short rains, from October to December. Rainy season does not, however, mean that it rains constantly during the said months, but that there are heavy showers, which are usually quite brief and frequently occur in the evenings, at night, or in the early morning. During the day the sun always retains the upper hand!

The climate on the coast is tropical. With annual rainfall of between

**Climatic Table**

**Comparison: Highlands (Nairobi) and Coast (Mombasa)**

| Months | Jan. | Feb. | Mar. | Apr. | May | June | July | Aug. | Sep. | Oct. | Nov. | Dec. |
|---|---|---|---|---|---|---|---|---|---|---|---|---|
| **Nairobi** | | | | | | | | | | | | |
| Daily high (° C) | 24 | 26 | 26 | 24 | 23 | 22 | 21 | 22 | 24 | 25 | 23 | 23 |
| Night-time low (° C) | 11 | 11 | 13 | 14 | 13 | 11 | 9 | 10 | 10 | 12 | 13 | 12 |
| Hours of sunshine | 9 | 9 | 8 | 7 | 6 | 6 | 4 | 4 | 6 | 7 | 7 | 8 |
| Water temperature (° C) | – | – | – | – | – | – | – | – | – | – | – | – |
| Humidity (%) | 50 | 43 | 47 | 57 | 62 | 56 | 58 | 55 | 49 | 46 | 56 | 57 |
| No. of rainy days* | 5 | 5 | 11 | 16 | 14 | 4 | 2 | 5 | 4 | 7 | 16 | 6 |
| **Mombasa** | | | | | | | | | | | | |
| Daily high (° C) | 32 | 32 | 33 | 31 | 29 | 29 | 28 | 28 | 29 | 30 | 31 | 32 |
| Night-time low (° C) | 23 | 23 | 24 | 24 | 23 | 23 | 22 | 22 | 22 | 22 | 23 | 23 |
| Hours of sunshine | 9 | 9 | 9 | 8 | 6 | 8 | 7 | 8 | 9 | 9 | 9 | 9 |
| Water temperature (° C) | 27 | 28 | 28 | 28 | 28 | 27 | 25 | 25 | 25 | 27 | 27 | 27 |
| Humidity (%) | 69 | 69 | 69 | 71 | 77 | 77 | 77 | 74 | 69 | 69 | 69 | 69 |
| No. of rainy days* | 4 | 2 | 5 | 10 | 14 | 9 | 11 | 10 | 9 | 12 | 10 | 9 |

*The number of rainy days indicates on how many days in a particular month it rains on average. Rain, however, usually takes the form of heavy but brief showers – you will rarely experience a continuous downpour.

700 and 1,300 mm (27–51 inches), average daily temperatures of 30 °C (86 °F) and nightly "lows" of 23 °C (73 °F), conditions can be very hot and sticky. The sultriness is alleviated somewhat by sea winds and by the monsoons known in East Africa as "kaskasi" and "kusi". The kaskasi blows from November to March and brings a pleasant coolness from the northeast. The beneficial effects of the kusi are to be felt from April to October.

The desert and semi-desert regions of Kenya (between the coastal strip and the highlands, near Ethiopia's border in the northeast, and around Lake Turkana in the northwest) remain hot and dry all year.

Most foreign visitors usually find Kenya at its best from December to March (conditions on the plateau are then hot and sunny), but June and July are also very pleasant, as are September and October. The latter is, by the way, the favourite month of the Kenyans themselves.

So, whereas Kenya used to be known as the ideal place for a winter holiday among people from the northern hemisphere ("Get away from the snow and into the sun!"), it has of late developed into a year-round destination.

# Vegetation

Mangrove swamps, savanna, montane forests, alpine vegetation, fertile farming land given over to intensive agriculture – the kinds of vegetation found in Kenya are as sharply defined as the divisions in the land's geographical make-up, and correspond with climatic conditions prevalent in each.

Although the predominate feature of vegetation in most of central Africa is the tropical rainforest (a belt of dense, evergreen forest stretches from the Gulf of Guinea, through the Congo basin and as far as the highlands mark the western boundary of the Great Rift Valley), this is not found to any substantial degree in Kenya.

The evergreen, broad-leaved trees of the rainforest need a "hothouse" climate in order to survive. Plentiful rainfall evenly distributed over the whole year (amounting to at least 1,500 mm/60 ins.) and a mean annual temperature of 25 °C (77 °F) are prerequisites. Climatic conditions in most of Kenya (i. e. a defined and extended dry season and marked fluctuations in daytime and night-time temperatures at any given time of year) preclude the presence of the rainforest there.

This is not to say that there are no dense tropical **forests** in Kenya. They do exist but only in isolation (on higher ground, near larger bodies of water, or as gallery forests along watercourses). Furthermore, the trees are no longer evergreen but **deciduous,** shedding their leaves at the onset of the dry season. The canopy they form is also lower than that of the rainforest, where the larger trees can reach a height of 50 m (164 ft).

A good example of such a lush tropical forest can be found at Kakamega, north of Kisumu on the shore of Lake Victoria. Here one can easily imagine oneself to be in the expansive rainforests of West Central Africa – the same impenetrable canopy, the intermediate trees and shrubs, and the undergrowth. As in the rainforest, epiphytes (mosses, orchids, etc.) are common here; and lianas of all thicknesses and lengths intertwine with branches and hang down like an Oriental curtain of twisted velvet cord.

Moving away from the margins of the rainforest and towards the arid plains, the length of the dry season increases and forests give way to ever sparser woodlands and eventually to grasslands. The **sparsely wooded savanna** so characteristic of Kenya is known in East Africa as "miombo". The landscape of short grasses and scattered trees is broken only be dense **gallery forests** which thrive alongside Kenya's major rivers (for example, along stretches of the Tana and Athi-Galana rivers).

Deciduous trees found in the forests of East Africa include acacias, baobabs and silk cotton trees. The acacia (also known as thorn tree because of the thorns which grow beside its compound leaves) is possibly *the* characteristic tree of the Kenyan savanna. **Acacias** are found either growing fairly densely along watercourses (where saplings usually have enough moisture to survive) or as isolated trees in drier areas (where the young trees are in greater danger of perishing due to lack of sufficient moisture). Once established, the acacias develop wide-spreading roots so as to be able to absorb sufficient moisture to survive the dry season. For the same reason compound leaves reduce evaporation to a minimum. The sharp thorns of the acacia protect the tree from possible damage caused by wild animals.

The **baobab** (Adansonia digitata, also known as the monkey bread tree) and the **silk cotton tree** (Ceiba pentendra, also known as the kapok tree) are both bombacaceous trees. This means that they have very thick stems and possess water-storing tissue which enables them to survive long periods of drought. The pulp of the fruit of the baobab – monkey bread – is edible. The baobab is able to store up to 120,000 litres of water in the soft wood of its thick trunk. Although the baobab can reach the ripe old age of 2,000 the soft trunk is often damaged by elephants. Kapok, used as a material for stuffing and for sound insulation, is in fact made of the yellowish white silky threads covering the seeds of the silk cotton tree.

Also to be found in Kenya, the balm of Gilead (Commiphora opobalsamum) is a burseraceous tree – it has compound leaves like the acacia, and the oily resin obtained

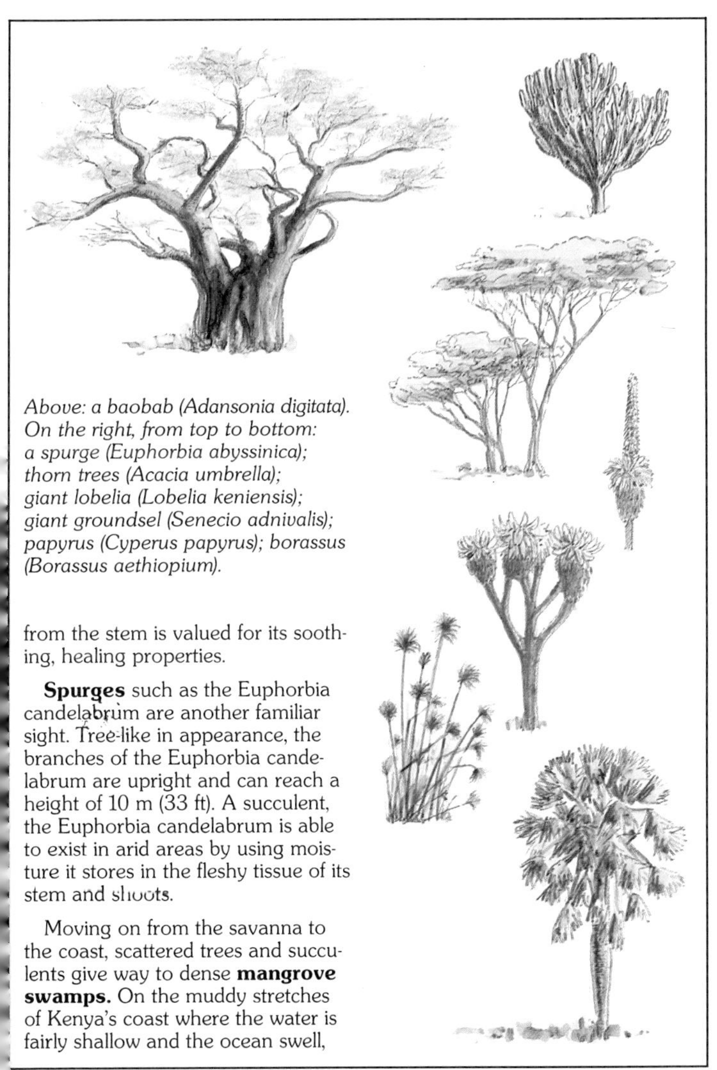

*Above: a baobab (Adansonia digitata). On the right, from top to bottom: a spurge (Euphorbia abyssinica); thorn trees (Acacia umbrella); giant lobelia (Lobelia keniensis); giant groundsel (Senecio adnivalis); papyrus (Cyperus papyrus); borassus (Borassus aethiopium).*

from the stem is valued for its soothing, healing properties.

**Spurges** such as the Euphorbia candelabrum are another familiar sight. Tree-like in appearance, the branches of the Euphorbia candelabrum are upright and can reach a height of 10 m (33 ft). A succulent, the Euphorbia candelabrum is able to exist in arid areas by using moisture it stores in the fleshy tissue of its stem and shoots.

Moving on from the savanna to the coast, scattered trees and succulents give way to dense **mangrove swamps.** On the muddy stretches of Kenya's coast where the water is fairly shallow and the ocean swell, not too strong, mangrove thickets are well established. The pneumatophores, specialized roots of the evergreen trees branch upwards and intertwine, and at low water their fantastic forms can be readily seen.

The most **varied vegetation** concentrated in one area is to be found in the **highlands** of Kenya, where altitude and rainfall make for clearly defined graduations as one moves towards higher ground.

At the foot of Mt. Kenya thorn-bush savanna gives way to more fertile areas which support denser growth. Where annual rainfall amounts to 1,000 mm (40 ins.) scrub and montane forest take over; then at 2,500 m (8,000 ft) bamboo forests predominate. 3,000 (10,000 ft) marks the limit of the true forest and at this altitude we find epiphytic and saprophytic plants (mosses, orchids, lichen, etc.). Giant St. John's wort (Hypericum) is also found here. Still higher we find a special kind of alpine vegetation peculiar to Africa – heath, giant lobelia (of which there are several species, some with white flowers, others with yellow or red or blue) and everlasting flowers (Helichrysum).

Since the first days of white settlement agriculturalists have taken advantage of the **fertile soil** and optimal climate of Kenya's interior to cultivate crops on land reclaimed from secondary forests or traditional pastures. Of particular importance today are coffee, tea, sugar cane and sisal in the fertile highlands, coconuts and sisal on the coast. Sisal, which is indiginous to Mexico and Central America, was introduced to East Africa at the end of the nineteenth century when it was brought to Tanganyika by the German East Africa Company.

Many different kinds of **flowers and trees** which flourish in tropical regions around the world are to be found in Kenya's town parks and gardens. The splendour of orchids, the brilliant red blossoms of flame trees, the pale pink to deep violet of the bougainvillea, the blue of the jacaranda... *(Nenzel)*

# Symbiosis in Bush and Savanna

The visitor to Kenya usually wants above all to see animals – wild animals roaming free in their natural habitat. In fact, more than 500,000 tourists from all over the world are attracted every year to the "wilderness" of East Africa. These visitors are rarely disappointed though, unfortunately, the creation of national parks and game reserves came too late to save many members of Africa's once so rich animal world.

If you go on one of today's safaris, you will most probably leave the palm-fringed beaches of Mombasa by air and reach Nairobi in the Highlands in just under an hour. Once there, you will be transported on good roads and tracks in comfortable buses and cross-country vehicles from one animal paradise to the next. Travelling in this way, it is almost impossible to imagine the hardships and dangers faced by explorers, traders and hunters less than a hundred years ago – before the Uganda railway was built – when they headed in the same direction from the coast to the interior. They, for their part, could hardly have imagined the profusion of wildlife awaiting them in the East African Highlands – the home of the world's most impressive big game herds.

Kenya's interior may be divided into three main regions. The first of these, the **scrub country** or "nyika" (wilderness), extends from the narrow, fertile coastal strip northwards to the watershed of the Tana river, and westwards as far as Mt. Kilimanjaro and the middle course of the Athi river. Next come the gently rolling **grassy plains** of the volcanic highlands, through which the lake basins and volcanic mountains of the Rift Valley run and which stretch almost as far as Lake Victoria and Lake Turkana. Finally, in a northerly direction, thorn scrub and grassland gradually give way to **desert regions,** which reach up to the borders with Somalia and Ethiopia and encompass almost half of Kenya.

## Thorn Scrub

At the turn of the century, travellers to East Africa arriving at the Indian Ocean coast needed about 15 days to cross the arduous and dangerous hurdle posed by the seemingly impenetrable thick thorn scrub and reach the open grasslands.

With the exception of during the short rainy season, the nyika is a dry, bleak and grey region with dense, thorny, low to medium-sized acacia trees and bushes, and scanty grass on usually sandy soils. The only plants to survive here are those which have adapted to resist drought and bushfires. Some have, for example, developed mechanisms which reduce transpiration; in others, specialized tissue in roots, nodules, stems, branches and leaves allows for storage of large amounts of moisture, or deep roots reach down to groundwater levels; others again are able to defoliate when conditions make this necessary.

The animals in the thorn scrub have also adapted to inhospitable living conditions. Masai giraffes, impalas, graceful gazelles, the lesser kudu and the black rhinoceros browse upon the foliage of bushes and trees, and buffaloes and zebras graze on the grassy areas near the few watering-places. It is here that lions and leopards lie in wait for their prey. What is particularly surprising about this barren landscape is the enormous variety of birds: there are all kinds of waxbills, weaver-birds, glossy starlings and falcons.

"Landscape designers" in the thorn scrub are the elephants. Over the large area in which they are found, they exercise nowhere more than here such a lasting influence on plant growth and thus on the lives of other animals. In the dry season elephant herds fell and clear the thorn trees to eat the foliage. The next bushfire removes the broken, dry branches and tree-trunks, and grasses germinate on the open areas thus created. In this way elephants convert bush into grassland, where grass-eating animals make their appearance until, after years, seedlings of bushes and trees regain the upper hand and the nyika returns.

The elephants in the thorn bush are also active as well-diggers, stamping deep holes in dried-up river beds until they reach the groundwater, and as road-builders, with their well-trodden trails from one watering-hole to the next. Elephants therefore help all other animals to survive in the dry bush.

**Grasslands**

When, after toiling on foot for weeks through the bush, with visibility often hardly more than 50 yards, the East African traveller of a hundred years ago suddenly came on grassy plains with thousands of wild animals grazing as far as the eye could see he must have thought he'd stepped from hell into heaven. The often unexpected switch from bush to grassland is probably attributable to the nature of the soil and not to climatic conditions. The huge East African grasslands evolved in the volcanic region of the African Rift Valley on ground consisting of layers of lava with shallow soils unsuitable for tree growth and on ground previously covered by lakes and swamps.

Plants found here include many different kinds of grasses (for example, red oats, penniselum, dog's-tooth grass) and herbaceous plants (species of clover and other papilionaceous plants). These provide valuable food for herbivores even when they are withered – one of the reasons for the rich animal life in the East African steppes.

Brindled gnus, often grazing together with zebras, form the huge herds of many thousands of migrating animals which are typical of this part of Africa. (Both seasonal changes and the search for food bring about such mass migrations.) The herds always employ the same trails, and these are deep-trodden after decades of use.

Hartebeests and other antelopes (kongonis, topis), Thomson's and Grant's gazelles, impalas, elands and Cape buffaloes belong to the animal society of the grasslands. These grasslands have developed over thousands of years, adapting to the grazing habits of hoofed animals.

Zebras, gnus and hartebeests eat the grass in various stages of its growth. They have a complementary effect, and do not contend with each other for food. First of all, the zebras consume the hard long grass. They are followed by brindled gnus, kongonis and gazelles, which prefer short grass. For their part, topis browse in swampy grasslands and bush on the withered stalks of fairly old grass scorned by other species. In addition to grass, impalas, gazelles and elands eat the foliage of bush-like acacias. Giraffes and black rhinoceroses live in gallery forests and thickets along water courses and on mountain slopes, where they can pull the leaves of acacia trees.

This grazing sequence adopted by the various hoofed animals ensures that the food offered by the grasslands is optimally utilized without damage to the environment.

For predators – lions, leopards, cheetahs, wild dogs, spotted hyenas, jackals – there is an abundant supply of animals in the East African grasslands. However, the big game has no appreciable influence on the stock of these animals – they only pounce on the weak and ailing herbivores which would not have survived the next drought anyway.

As a result of this beasts of prey do not multiply disproportionately in the grasslands. In the Nairobi National Park, for instance, there are only about twenty lions to four or five thousand large hoofed animals.

Lion packs stay on their established hunting grounds and will not tolerate the presence of any strange lion. When the hoofed herds pass on, the big cats do not follow them and food then becomes scarce.

Whereas the cheetah hunts gazelles in the open steppes, relying on his incredible speed over short distances, the leopard lies in wait in thickets and gallery forests for baboons, impalas and smaller antelopes. Spotted hyenas are by no means only scavengers, but highly active hunters too. In packs they will snatch the newly-born young of many steppe animals and kill even zebras in packs and old, weak lions. African wild dogs roam in packs and trail, as hunters, the herds of migrating animals.

Jackals, hyenas, vultures, marabous and finally ants and other insects remove the carrion of herbivorous animals which have been killed or have perished as a result of drought or disease.

The flora and fauna in the East African savannas thus live in a state of biological equilibrium – unless, that is, this delicate balance is destroyed by man.

**Semi-Deserts in the North**

North of the Tana river, the Mt. Kenya massif and the Laikipia Steppe, thorn scrub and grasslands turn into the arid regions of the Somali highlands, semi-deserts with sandy or laval soils and but the scantiest vegetation. Where low acacias, balm of Gilead trees and acanthus bushes are found, succulents such as aloes, spurges and crassulaceous plants also thrive.

In Kenya's barren northern provinces, which beyond the Samburu National Reserve and Lake Baringo are hardly touched by tourism at all, animal species can be found which do not occur in the thorn scrub and grasslands. These include Grévy's zebra (almost extinct as a result of poaching), the Eritrean buck, the northern giraffe gazelle, greater and lesser kudu, Hunter's antelope and marvellous reticulated giraffe.

The western boundary of this area is formed by the 240 km (150 mile) long and up to 50 km (31 mile) wide Lake Turkana. Lake Turkana teems with Nile crocodiles, some of them the biggest which have ever gone down on record. They feed – as the numerous pink pelicans do – exclusively on Nile perch and other fish.

Huge flocks of ducks, geese, ibis, spoonbills and cormorants live on the shores of Kenya's lakes. In addition, the sight of huge flocks of flamingo on the lakes is truly magnificent.

*(Wünschmann)*

# Kenya's Wildlife

Of the 1,500 species of mammal present in Africa, some 100 are now to be found in Kenya. Among these there are close to 40 different ungulates or hoofed mammals (in Central Europe there are only 7 species of ungulate). In addition, Kenya boasts 1,000 species of bird – experienced ornithologists will probably sight 200 of these in a single day's observation. For any non-specialist wishing to study East African wildlife closely, the books listed below can be recommended.

– T. Haltenorth and H. Diller, A Field Guide to the Mammals of Africa (Collins, London)
– J. Dorst and P. Dandelot, A Field Guide to the Larger Mammals of Africa (Collins, London)
– J. G. Williams and N. Arlott, A Field Guide to the Birds of East Africa (Collins, London)
– J. G. Williams and N. Arlott, A Field Guide to the National Parks of East Africa (Collins, London)

The following summary offers a small selection of the animals you are likely to encounter in East Africa.

Baboon
*(Puplo cynocephalus)*

Vervet or Green Monkey
*(Cercopithecus aethiops)*

Sykes Monkey
*(Cercopithecus albogularis)*

## Mammals

### 1. Monkeys and Prosimians

**Anubis Baboon**
Large, long-tailed, heavily-built monkey (body length up to 100 cm); olive brown; omnivorous; mainly terrestrial; diurnal and sociable (troops of 20–80 animals under leadership of the dominant male). Habitat: Widespread in open areas of Kenya.

**Vervet or Green Monkey**
Medium-sized (body length 40–80 cm); slender, long-tailed; general colour greyish, or yellowish-olive; black face surrounded by white hair; testes bright blue; omnivorous, mainly vegetarian; arboreal and terrestrial; diurnal and sociable (family bands of 10–50 animals). Habitat: Widespread in humid and dry savannas, thornbush, fringing forests and bushes – always near water.

**Sykes Monkey**
Medium-sized (body length 50–70 cm), stoutly-built, long-tailed monkey; olive-brown to greyish-black; throat, ears and forehead white; arboreal, sociable in family bands; Diet: Fruits, leaves, young shoots. Habitat: Montane forests, gallery forests, wooded savannas.

**Guereza**
Large (body length up to 80 cm), heavily-built, long-tailed monkey; naked face; jet black with white beard and whiskers and a conspicuous pure white mantle extending along the flanks from shoulders to tail; basal part of tail black, terminal part bushy white. (Colobus monkeys were long hunted for their attractive coat – highly prized during the last century.) Colobus means "mutilated" – these monkeys have only four fingers, the thumb being vestigial or absent. Arboreal; diurnal and sociable (family troops 3–18 individuals) living in feeding territories of variable size (8–15 hectares) depending on the number of animals. Diet: Specialized on fresh leaves, young shoots and fruits. Habitat: Montane and gallery forests (up to 3,000 m).

**Galago or Bushbaby**
Two species in Kenya: the small grey Senegal galago, body length 15–22 cm, and the larger, brown, thick-tailed galago, body length 30–45 cm. The bushy tail is longer than the body. Nocturnal prosimians (large eyes and ears), very active and fast-moving (leaping 7 m), well adapted to arboreal life; very variable calls, some like those of a crying baby. Diet: Insects, spiders, small vertebrates, also fruits, seeds, leaves, young shoots. Habitat: Bush country and tree savannas; sometimes more than 100 individuals per sq. km.

**Black and White Colobus**
***(Colobus guereza)***

**Senegal Bushbaby**
***(Galago senegalensis)***

Lion, "Simba"
*(Panthera leo)*

## 2. Carnivores

### Lion

Only sociable big cat, living and hunting in prides (1–3 adult males, up to 15 females and young). Adult males demarcate and defend their territory. Though hunting mainly early or at night, lions are more diurnal than other cats. Naturally lazy, they spend most of the day resting under trees and bushes. Hunting in groups (mainly lionesses), they approach the quarry by crouching low on the ground (often near waterholes), springing on its back and breaking its neck or killing by strangulation. They prey on various herbivorous animals ranging from small antilopes to hartebeest, wildebeest, zebra, giraffe, buffalo, but do not refuse carrion and sometimes even snatch away hyaenas' prey. Gestation period 102–113 days, average 2–3 cubs per litter, weaned at 10 weeks, independent and able to hunt after 18–20 months. Habitat: Open and sparsely-wooded grasslands, bush, semi-desert.

### Leopard

Numerous black spots and "rosettes" on buff or tawny coat; body length 110–160 cm, tail 60–100 cm. Diurnal and nocturnal, usually solitary big cat; home range and hunting territory 5–10 sq. km. Prey: All mammals up to medium-sized antilopes, preferably monkeys, but also dogs, goats, sheep, birds and reptiles. Prey generally seized by the neck. Leopards often carry their prey into a tree. Habitat: Everything from dense forests, gallery forests and rocky areas to dry open country and semi-deserts.

Having been hunted for their valuable fur, leopards have become rare in most parts of Africa, but they are recovering, since export, import and trade of big cat pelts are banned under the "Washington Convention" (CITES).

### Cheetah

Swiftest mammal; small head and very long thin legs (body length 110–140 cm, tail 70–80 cm, shoulder height 75 cm); numerous small round black spots on tawny coat. Cheetahs live singly or in small groups (mother with young), hunting mostly in the morning and evening. Unlike other cats they run down their quarry in rapid sprint (up to 120 km. p. h.) over short distances, seizing prey by the throat. Prey: Gazelles and other smaller or young antelopes, birds. Habitat: Open and semi-arid savannas.

Hunted for their pelts, they are endangered but are now protected under the "Washington Convention" (CITES).

### Serval

Medium-sized, long-legged cat (body length 65–90 cm, tail 25–35 cm); coat yellowish brown with black spots, bands and stripes. Diurnal, solitary animal. Prey: Smaller mammals, birds, reptiles, – approached as closely as possible, birds taking wing seized in high jump. Habitat: Open savannas, bush, always near water.

### Spotted Hyaena

Powerfully built, sloping back, body length 120–180 cm; broad and massive head with strong teeth; irregular dark brown spots on buff colour; fairly short tail, bushy black tip. Sociable animals (packs of 10–30, sometimes up to 100 individuals), but also singly or in pairs. Territorial but also follow migrating herds of hoofed animals. Mainly nocturnal. Very noisy, several types of cry (low hoarse tones rising to high-pitched screams, "laughter"). Scavengers feeding mainly on carrion, but also hunt game and cattle in packs. Prey brought down by biting legs and ankles, lacerated alive and eaten completely. Hyenas swallow huge pieces of meat and bones, their powerful jaws cracking even large bones and extracting the marrow.

### Wild Dog

Size and features of a slender, long-legged dog (body 80–108 cm); massive head and broad ears; coat very variable, with black, dark brown, yellow and white patches; bushy tail with conspicuous white tip. Wild dogs are diurnal; in packs they roam about in pursuit of the migrating herds of ungulates; they pursue prey (antelopes, zebras) in an organised manner, alternating with each other, biting where they can, snapping out portions of flesh until the victim falls, then lacerating it, sometimes still alive, within a few minutes. Habitat: Open and wooded savanna, also semi-desert, up to high mountains; numbers decreasing all over Africa.

### Jackals

Fox-sized, but longer legs (body length 70–100 cm, tail 25–40 cm); three species in Kenya: black-backed jackal with dark mantle on upperparts, side-striped jackal with whitish stripe along flank, common jackal yellowish with some blackish on upperparts. Jackals pair for life; mainly nocturnal, territorial. Prey: Small animals of all kinds, carrion, afterbirth of hoofed animals. Habitat: Open and wooded savanna, bush country.

Leopard, "Chui"
(Panthera pardus)
Serval
(Felis serval)
Cheetah, "Duma"
(Acinonyx jubatus)

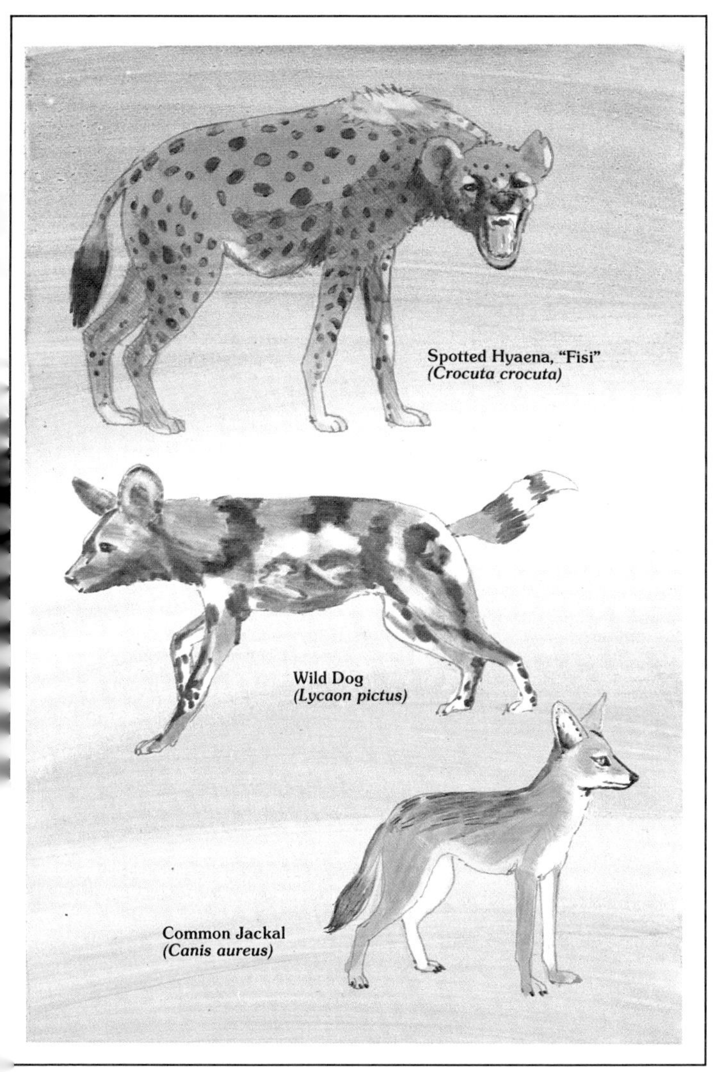
Spotted Hyaena, "Fisi"
(Crocuta crocuta)
Wild Dog
(Lycaon pictus)
Common Jackal
(Canis aureus)

## 3. Hyrax and Elephants

### Tree Hyrax, Rock Hyrax and Yellow-Spotted Hyrax

Small, robust animals resembling marmots, but forming a distinct order being more closely related to the elephant than other ungulates (teeth, toe nails, sole pads and other anatomical features). Sociable, well adapted to climbing, exclusively

**Rock Dassie, "Pimbi"**
***(Procavia capensis)***

vegetarian. Habitat: Forests (tree hyrax); scrub-covered rocky places in savanna and bush (rock and yellow-spotted hyrax).

### African Bush Elephant

Largest living land mammal (height 3–4 m, weight 4.5–6 t); large ears; tusks both in bulls (length up to 345 cm) and cows (up to 75 cm); size of tusks decreasing (selective shooting by ivory hunters). Gestation about 22 months; fully adult at 10 or 12; life span up to 60 years (depending on the wear of the molar teeth, the sixth and last set of which is produced at the age of 30–35 years). Family units (10–20 individuals) under leadership of an old female; bulls live in bachelor groups, old bulls also solitary. On their seasonal migrations elephants unite in large herds (sometimes hundreds of animals). Highly-developed social behaviour, helping each other when giving birth or when a member of the herd is wounded or sick. When the cows are in heat (oestrous cycle 2–3 weeks), adult bulls join the females. Sense of sight not very developed, but scent and hearing excellent. Diet: Leaves, twigs, terminal shoots, bark, roots, fruits, long grass (up to 80% of the diet) and domestic crops. Daily food consumption 100–200 kg (feeding constantly), water 100–300 litres. Very flexible trunk used for collecting food, sucking up water, transferring to mouth. Daily bathing, covering body with mud or dust afterwards protects against sun and insects. Habitat: Formerly in savannas and gallery forests, migrating to grassland and semi-desert during rainy season; today habitat threatened by man. When concentrated in national parks and reserves, elephant populations have to be controlled to avoid landscape destruction. During the last 20 years Kenya's elephants have decreased in number by more than 50% to about 60,000, due to loss of habitat, drought and ivory poaching.

African Elephant, "Tembo"
*(Loxodonta africana)*

## 4. Odd-Toed Ungulates

### Black Rhinoceros

Two fibrous horns of dermal origin on the nose, anterior horn longer (50–80 cm, max. 120 cm) than the posterior (30–40 cm, max. 60 cm). Body length 300–360 cm, weight 700–1,600 kg. Tridactyl feet with three hooves. Senses of smell and hearing excellent, sight poor. Rhinos

**Black Rhinoceros, "Faru"**
***(Diceros bicormis)***

are active mostly in the morning and at dusk, resting during the day; usually solitary. Gestation period about 15 months; one calf born at a time, weaned at 1 year, sexually mature at 6–7 years, life span up to 40 years. Diet: Leaves, buds, twigs, young shoots, being picked with pointed prehensile upper lip. Habitat: Dry bush country, thorn scrub, edge of forests, mountain moorland.

Rhinos are among those animals most severely endangered by poaching (in traditional East Asian medicine rhino horn is believed to have special properties). During the last 20 years rhinos in Kenya have been decimated; their numbers reduced by more than 90% to less than 1,000 specimens.

### Grant's Zebra

Broad black stripes down to hooves; body length 200–240 cm; small ears. Sociable; family troops consisting of the leading stallion and 1 to 6 mares with foals; young stallions in bachelor herds; on migration during the dry season family groups assemble in large herds, often with wildebeest and other antelopes. Diet: Mainly tough long grass. Habitat: Open grassy plains and well grassed woodland. Enemies: Lion, spotted hyaena, wild dog.

### Grevy's Zebra

Largest of the wild equids (body length 250–260 cm); narrow black stripes down to hooves, underparts white; broad brown spinal stripe from middle of back to tail; broad rounded ears. Sociable, groups of mares with foals; stallions solitary (territorial) or in groups; sometimes with oryx or wildebeest. Diet: Mainly grass; they paw waterholes in dry river beds. Habitat: Restricted to the north of Kenya, in arid bushland and semi-desert. Population threatened and reduced by poaching. Enemies: Lion, spotted hyaena, wild dog.

Grant's Zebra, "Punda milia"
*(Equus burchelli granti)*
Grevy's Zebra
*(Hippotigris grevyi)*

## 5. Even-Toed Ungulates

### Hippopotamus

Huge animal; heavy barrel-shaped rump (body length 320–340 cm, weight 1.5–3.2 t); short legs, four-toed webbed feet; enormous head, extremely broad muzzle, long curved canine tusks (up to 100 cm); nostrils and ears closed when submerged.

Very sociable; family herds 5 to 15, sometimes up to 30 individuals led by an old bull; young bulls are expelled from the herd until old enough (at 8–10 years) to fight with older bulls for territory. Habitat: Streams, lakes and ponds with shallows banks bordered by grassland (feeding range). Territory demarcated by dominant bull (disperses excreta) and defended against rivals in fierce fights. Truly amphibious, well adapted to living in water, feeding at night on land. Hippos can dive for 1–5 mins, sometimes even 15 mins. They give birth in shallow water (gestation period about 235 days, calves weaned after one year).

### Warthog

Coat sparse and bristly, long stiff hairs on neck and shoulders, whiskers, broad head with large warts; body length 110–150 cm; curved canine tusks (up to 60 cm). Diet: Grass, fruits, roots, bulbs; often "kneeling" to graze.

Sociable animal, living in family parties, old males solitary; diurnal; territorial, sleeping and breeding in enlarged aardvark burrows or other sheltered hollows. Habitat: Open savanna. Enemies: Lion, leopard.

### Giraffe

Height (top of head) 450–580 cm, weight 500–800 kg. 2–5 "horns" covered with skin and hairs on forehead and occiput, used for blows in fights among males. Two subspecies in Kenya: the reticulated giraffe in the north (deep chestnut brown with network of narrow light lines) and the Masai giraffe (with dark brown, vine-leaf-like irregular patches on light brown). Sociable without strict hierarchy, herds of 3–40 individuals, bulls also in herds or solitary. Habitat: Dry savannas, gallery forests. Diet: Leaves and twigs (especially acacias) collecting food with long prehensile upper lip and tongue. When drinking, bring head down to water by spreading forelegs. Gestation period 440 days, female giving birth in standing position. Territorial fights among males, standing side by side, striking with neck and head. Enemies (even lions) are repulsed by well-aimed hoof blows.

### African Buffalo

Only African representative of wild cattle. Body length 265 cm; height 165 cm; weight 800 kg; bulls larger and heavier than cows. Generally black, adults have sparse coat, old animals nearly hairless; heavy horns with massive base, much bigger in males (spanning up to 150 cm). Gregarious, herds of 20–2,000 animals, no distinct hierarchy, cows with calves often separate from bulls, old bulls solitary and territorial. Buffalos defend themselves and their calves fiercely, even lions may be wounded or killed; when shot or cornered old bulls can be dangerous to man. Habitat: Open plains, near water.

Reticulated Giraffe, "Twiga"
*(Giraffa c. reticulata)*
Warthog, "Ngiri"
*(Phacochoerus aethiopicus)*
Masai Giraffe, "Twiga"
*(Giraffa c. tippelskirchi)*
African Buffalo, "Mbogo"
*(Syncerus caffer)*
Hippopotamus, "Kiboko"
*(Hippopotamus amphibius)*

**White-Bearded Gnu or Wildebeest**

Large antelope (body length 180–240 cm), heavily built, massive head with broad muzzle and horns (both sexes) curving downwards then upwards; hindquarters slender, limbs thin. Coat grey with dark bands on foreparts; black hairs on face; white beard on throat; black mane on neck and shoulders; black tuft of tail nearly reaches ground. Gregarious, seen either in territorial breeding groups of 6–20 females herded by one bull, in bachelor troops or in large wandering herds, often with zebras and gazelles. 80% of the calves are born within a period of 2–3 weeks, in Kenya usually in January and February; in large herds the loss of young to carnivores is less (15%) than in smaller herds (up to 50%). About 400,000 wildebeest migrate between the Mara and Serengeti plains. Diet: Short grasses. Enemies: Lion, leopard, spotted hyaena, wild dog. Habitat: Open plains, bush country.

**Kongoni or Coke's Hartebeest**

Size like gnu (body length 175–245 cm), but more slender; uniform sandy colour; ridged horns (both sexes) curved upwards. Gregarious; territorial breeding groups (3–10 individuals), bachelor troops, during dry season also large herds, sometimes with zebras. Diet: Grasses and herbs. Habitat: Grassy plains, savanna, woodland. Nearly extinct in central Kenya.

**Topi**

Somewhat smaller than gnu (body length 150–205 cm), slender; colour rufous with blackish patches on face, shoulders, upper forelegs, hips and thighs; ridged horns (both sexes) thick, lyrate, slightly curved upwards. Gregarious; small territorial breeding groups, dominant males guarding herd and territory in typical "watching position" on slight elevation; in dry season topis gather in large herds of several hundred often with other antelopes, zebras, ostriches. Diet: Grass and herbs. Habitat: Grassy plains, woodland, bush, also flooded areas.

**Waterbuck**

Medium-sized (body length 180–220 cm), heavily built. Ridged horns in males only, curving backwards and upwards, up to 90 cm long. Shaggy, water-repellent coat, grey to brown; buttocks pure white (Defassa waterbuck) or dark and surrounded by conspicuous white ring (common waterbuck); in Kenya usually intermediate form. Old males solitary and territorial throughout the year; groups of females and young, and separate bachelor troops roam about. Habitat: Grasslands with bushes and gallery woodland, never far from water; flight to water and reeds. Diet: Grasses left by other grazers, leaves, tender shoots. Enemies: Lion, leopard, wild dog (only when other prey not available; waterbuck have strong musky odour and tough, fibrous meat).

**Bohor Reedbuck**

Small antelope (body length 120–140 cm); short horns (males only), tips curve forewards; yellowish-brown coat; short bushy tail. Live singly, in pairs, or in small family parties (6–12); territorial, one adult male defending territory. Shrill whistle when alarmed, bolting from cover only at the last moment. Diet: Mainly grasses. Habitat: Grassland, swamps with bushes and reeds. Enemies: All major predators.

**Beisa Oryx**
Large antelope (body length 160–235 cm); horns (both sexes) long (up to 120 cm), straight, heavily-ridged, slightly curved. Colour fawn with well-defined black-and-white pattern on head, rump and legs; subspecies in southern Kenya with tufted ears. Orys live in pairs or family troops, old bulls also singly; non-territorial. Habitat: Dry, open bush, short-grass savanna, semi-desert, often far from water. Diet: Coarse grasses, shrubs, succulent plants. In Kenya, found in the north (Samburu, Marsabit) and in the south (Amboseli, Tsavo). Enemies: Lion, leopard, wild dog, but oryx pugnacious when attacked, impaling even lions with their horns.

**Eland**
Very large antelope (body length 240–320 cm), height up to 170 cm, weight 1 t), ox-like appearance, but more slender. Horns with tight spiral, in bulls up to 100 cm long and massive. Colour fawn or tawny to rufous, with narrow white vertical stripes on rump; dewlap with tuft of black hairs. Gregarious, living in troops of 6–30 individuals, sometimes in larger herds; old bulls also solitary. Habitat: Open plains and savanna. Diet: Grasses, herbs, leaves, fruits, bulbs, tuberous roots. Enemies: Lion, wild dog.

**Lesser Kudu**
Very graceful, medium-sized antilope (body length 120–140 cm); large funnel-shaped ears; only male has spiral horns (up to 90 cm). Adult males are brownish-grey to blue-grey, females reddish-fawn, both with 11–15 narrow, white vertical stripes on flanks. Lesser kudu live singly, in pairs or in small troops; territorial. Habitat: Characteristic of semi-arid bush country ("Njika"), but never common. Diet: Leaves, young shoots. Enemies: Leopard, wild dog.

**Bushbuck**
Medium-sized antelope (body length 120–150 cm); short, slightly spiralled horns (males only); coloration and coat pattern very variable (chestnut to grey-brown with white stripes and/or spots). Bushbuck are territorial, living singly or in pairs. Habitat: Forest thickets, dense bush, also in agriculture areas, not far from water. Diet: Leaves, tender shoots, pods, also tubers and roots. Enemy: Leopard; barking alarm call.

**Impala**
Medium-sized (body 120–160 cm), slight, very graceful antelope; horns (males only) slender, lyrate, up to 90 cm long. Smooth coat, reddish-brown to fawn, paler on flanks, underparts white; tuft of black hairs above heels of hind legs. Gregarious, territorial; living in family groups, each dominant buck with 10–30 females, demarcating and defending territory; young bucks roam about in bachelor troops. Habitat: Savanna, woodlands, often near water. Diet: Short grasses and

Wildebeest or White-Bearded Gnu, "Nyumbo ya montu"
(Connochaetes taurinus)
Coke's Hartebeest, "Kongoni"
(Alcelaphus buselaphus)
Common Waterbuck, "Kuru"
(Kobus ellipsiprymnus)
Bohor Reedbuck, "Tohe"
(Redunca redunca)
Topi, "Nyamera"
(Damaliscus lunatus)

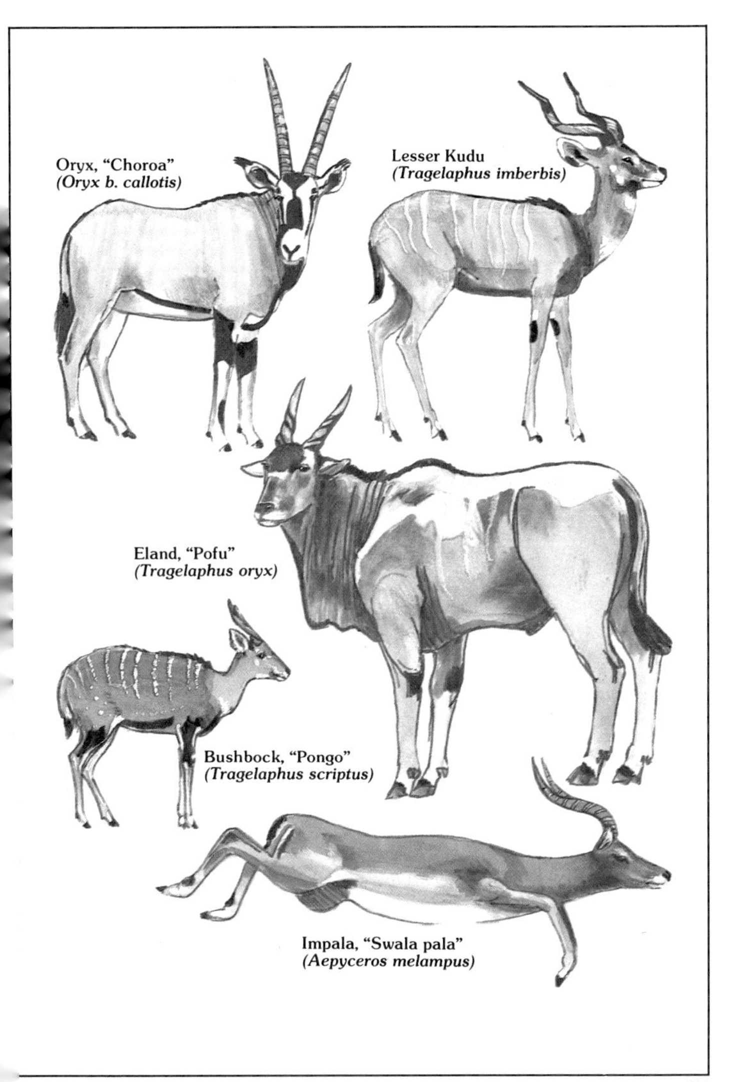
Oryx, "Choroa"
*(Oryx b. callotis)*
Lesser Kudu
*(Tragelaphus imberbis)*
Eland, "Pofu"
*(Tragelaphus oryx)*
Bushbock, "Pongo"
*(Tragelaphus scriptus)*
Impala, "Swala pala"
*(Aepyceros melampus)*

leaves. Enemies: Leopard, cheetah, lion, wild dog, spotted hyaena, nile crocodile.

**Grant's Gazelle**
Size similar to impala; fawn with white underparts and buttocks; lyrate horns curving backwards (80 cm long in males, 30–40 cm in females). Adult bucks defend territories in which they try to herd a group of 6–30 females; young males forming bachelor troops; during the dry season large herds (40–400 animals) migrate, some times with other ungulates.

Habitat: Open plains, bush, in northern Kenya also semi-deserts. Diet: Grasses and leaves. Enemies: Leopard, cheetah, wild dog, lion.

**Thomson's Gazelle**
Smaller than Grant's gazelle (body length 90–110 cm), very graceful. Lyrate, short horns, curve backwards slightly (in males 25–40, in females 7–15 cm long). Fawn with white underparts and broad black lateral band (most conspicuous feature). Gregarious; loosely organized and variable herd structure: harem groups (10–70), mother-young parties, bachelor troops (up to 500). In the dry season large herds (several thousand) gather, often with gnus, Grant's gazelles, zebras. Diet: Mainly grasses.

Habitat: Grass plains and open bush country. The commonest gazelle in East Africa (also outside game reserves). Enemies: Major predators, also jackal, baboon, eagle, python.

**Gerenuk**
Large, graceful, long-limbed and extremely long-necked gazelle (length from head to tail 140–160 cm); small head; horns (males only) thick, heavily ringed, S-shaped, curved backwards (25–44 cm). Smooth coat, reddish-brown, upper back darker, underparts white. Territorial, sociable; small family parties or pairs, sometimes with Grant's gazelles or beisa oryx.

Habitat: Bush country and semi-desert, common nowhere. Diet: Browses on leaves, tender shoots, buds and fruits, often standing on hind legs when eating. Enemies: Leopard, but also cheetah, wild dog, lion.

**Klipspringer**
Small antelope (body length 75–115 cm); thick, coarse coat olive brown speckled with grey; short pointed horns (males only). Pair for life, live as pairs or small family parties; territorial.

Habitat: Rocky hills with bush and scrub shelter, savanna, semi-desert and mountains. Springs on tips of hooves. Diet: Leaves, herbs, grasses. Enemies: Leopard, caracal, serval, eagles.

**Kirk's Dik-Dik**
Smallest antelope; hare-sized (body-length 55–70 cm), delicate; elongated nose; large eyes; tuft of hairs on forehead; grey to greyish-brown. Live in pairs in defined territories.

Habitat: Dry bush country with thicket shelter. Diet: Leaves, young shoots, buds, blossoms, herbs. Enemies: Medium-sized predators, eagles, pythons.

Kirk's Dik-Dik, "Dikidiki"
*(Madoqua kirki)*

Grant's Gazelle, "Swala granti"
*(Gazella granti)*

Thomson's Gazelle,
"Swala tomi"
*(Gazella thomsoni)*

Giraffe-Gazelle or Gerenuk,
"Swala twiga"
*(Litocranius walleri)*

Klipspringer, "Ngurunguru"
*(Oreotragus oreotragus)*

**Birds**

## 1. Ostriches

At 2.60 m and 150 kg the ostrich is the largest living bird. Powerful legs, only two toes (the largest with a strong nail); a fast, tenacious runner, speeds up to 65 km p. h., stride 4 m. Sociable; large flocks of 20–100 individuals (except during breeding period) often with hoofed animals. Mating and breeding during rainy season; usually one adult male with senior hen and 2–3 subordinates, together laying about 20 eggs (weight up to 1.5 kg) in common nest, a rough hollow in the ground. Both cock and hen incubate eggs, the inconspicuous hen by day, the black-and-white cock at night; incubation 6 weeks. Habitat: Savanna, bush, semi-desert. Diet: Grasses, fruits, insects, small animals. Distribution: Somali ostrich in northern Kenya (blue-grey neck and legs in males); Masai ostrich in central and southern Kenya (neck and legs flesh-coloured). Population still safe.

## 2. Totipalmate Swimmers

### Cormorants
Dark-plumaged, slender, long-necked waterbirds with hooked bills, swimming and diving to capture food, mainly fish and amphibians. Two species in East Africa: white-necked cormorant, long-tailed cormorant. Sociable, breeding colonies found on all suitable inland waters.

### African Darter
Cormorant-like, but larger; very long neck, bill sharply pointed (instead of hooked). Darters swim very low in water with only head and neck showing, resembling snake, hence name "snakebird". With a sharp stab fish are impaled on bill. Once out of the water, cormorants and darters dry outstretched wings in the sun.

### Pelicans
Very large water birds with large bills and distensible pouches. Two species in East Africa: great white pelican and pink-backed pelican (smaller, pale grey), both abundant on Rift Valley lakes. Sociable, breeding in colonies. Tactical fishers, at times they form a semi-circle, driving fish into shallow water where they catch them with ease using the pouches of their bills as scoops.

## 3. Herons and Egrets

Medium-sized or tall wading birds, usually with a nape-crest. About 14 species in East Africa. In flight the head is tucked back between shoulders with neck curved, distinguishing them from cranes, etc. Habitat: Lake shores, wetlands. Diet: Fish, amphibians, insects, reptiles and small mammals.

### Goliath Heron
Largest heron, standing 1.40 m; grey upperparts, rufous head, neck and underparts.

### Black-Headed Heron
Grey, black crown, neck, crest and legs; white throat. Approx. 1 m in height. Often found away from water hunting insects and mice.

**Great White Egret**
Large, white; long yellow bill, long nape-crest, black legs and feet.

**Yellow-Billed Egret**
White, smaller than great white egret, short yellow bill, black legs and feet.

**Little Egret**
Much smaller than other egrets, dazzling white, long mantle feathers, long black bill and legs.

**Cattle Egret**
White plumage, buff plumes on crown, chest and back; yellow bill, flesh-coloured legs. Smaller, more thickset and shorter-legged than little egret. Flocks accompany large game and cattle herds. Most common egret species, also found near human settlements; has now spread to other tropical countries.

## 4. Storks and Ibises

Tall or medium-sized wading birds, excellent gliders (necks extended in flight, not drawn back as in herons, egrets). Habitat: Savanna, wetlands. Diet: Small animals, insects, reptiles, amphibians. Of the 14 species found in East Africa:

**Saddle-Billed Stork**
Largest stork in Africa (height 1.50 m, wing span 2.40 m). Head, neck, mantle and tail black, irides-cent with green, violet and blue, rest of pluming white; bill red and black with yellow frontal saddle. Lives singly or in pairs.

**Abdim's Stork**
Medium-sized, glossy black stork, white belly. Often found in very large flocks following migratory locusts in grasslands and semi-deserts.

**Marabou Stork**
Large stork; strong heavy bill; head, neck and large pouch at front of neck bald (pouch consists of series of air sacs); white underparts, otherwise dark plumage. Scavenger feeding on refuse and carrion; found near water, in grasslands and settled areas. Sociable, breeding in colonies.

**Yellow-Billed Stork**
Medium-sized, pale pink and black; ochre bill curves downwards. Inland waters and coasts; breeds in colonies.

**Open-Billed Stork**
Medium-sized, black; wide gap between upper and lower mandibles when closed, adapted for feeding on certain large shellfish.

**Hammerkop**
Small, dusky brown; crest at back of head; lives singly or in pairs in swamps and shallow waters; builds huge closed nest, mostly of sticks, in fork of a tree, 5–12 m above ground, small entrance hole in side.

**Sacred Ibis**
Medium-sized; plumage mainly white, ornamental feathers on lower back, wings black; head and neck bald, black; bill and legs black. Common in wetlands and pasture-land.

**Hadada Ibis**
Medium-sized; grey-green with glossy green wing coverts. Found in wetlands, on lakes, river banks, pastureland. Typical call "ha-da-da".

**African Spoonbill**
Medium-sized; white plumage, red face and legs; characteristic spatulate bill used for feeding on insects, molluscs and worms in mud and shallow water.

## 5. Flamingos

Long-legged, long-necked wading birds; mainly pink and white. Highly specialized bill, flattened above with the tip at an angle, filters algae, crustaceans, insect larva (abundant in brackish waters of East Africa's lakes) from shallow water and mud. Lesser flamingos nowhere more plentiful than in Rift Valley (1.5–2 million breeding in vast colonies on lakes). The larger, paler-coloured greater flamingo less common (main nesting place India) but also found.

## 6. Ducks and Geese

Less abundant in East Africa than in Europe. Some typical species:

**Egyptian Goose**
Medium-sized; pale brown with white shoulders conspicuous in flight. In pairs or small flocks, common on all East African inland waters.

**Spur-Winged Goose**
Large goose; glossy black upperparts, white belly, red bill and bare face, shoulder tipped with a spur. In pairs or small flocks, often in savanna far from water.

**Knob-Billed Goose**
Medium-sized; glossy black upperparts; neck and underparts white; knob at base of drake's bill; grey head. Swamps and lakes (e. g. Lake Naivasha).

**White-Faced Tree Duck**
Small and slender; mainly chestnut-brown with conspicuous white face, black neck and bill. Tree ducks stand more erect than other ducks.

**Cape Wigeon**
Generally speckled greyish-brown, bright red bill.

**Red-Billed Duck**
Generally dusky brown with dark brown hood, pale cheeks and red bill.

**Yellow-Billed Duck**
A rather large grey-brown duck with metallic green wing speculum and conspicuous yellow bill.

**Hottentot Teal**
Smallest East African duck; dark brown with blackish-brown hood, pale cheeks and bluish bill.

## 7. Birds of Prey

**Secretary Bird**
Large, slender, long-legged; pale grey with black flight feathers, long tail and conspicuous crest feathers. Usually seen in pairs on plains and grasslands looking for snakes, other reptiles and small mammals.

1. Saddle-Billed Stork
(Ephippiorhynchus senegalensis)
2. Yellow-Billed Stork
(Ibis ibis)
3. Sacred Ibis
(Threskiornis aethiopicus)
4. Lesser Flamingo
(Phoenicopterus minor)
5. African Spoonbill
(Platalea alba)
6. Secretary Bird
(Sagittarius serpentarius)
1.
2.
3.
4.
5.
6.
Ostrich
(Struthio camelus)

**White-Backed Vulture**
Dark or pale brown, medium-sized, most common vulture in East Africa; nests in trees.

**Rüppel's Griffon Vulture**
Large, dark brown vulture, creamy-white edges of feathers lend scaly appearance; nests in tall trees and on cliffs.

**White-Headed Vulture**
Medium-sized with woolly white head and neck, red bill; otherwise blackish-brown. Singly or in pairs; kills living prey occasionally.

**Lappet-Faced Vulture**
Very large, mainly dark brown vulture with bald red head; also kills living prey; nests in cliffs.

**Egyptian Vulture**
Small, slender; white with black flight feathers; yellow, naked face, narrow bill. Adaptable, often found near human settlements feeding on refuse.

**Hooded Vulture**
Small, slender; dark brown; slender bill; over much of Africa, also near man, living on refuse and offal.

Of the more than 50 species of falcons, kites, eagles, buzzards, hawks and harriers found in East Africa, a few examples:

**Tawny Eagle**
Medium-sized, brown; common on all open plains and in cultivated areas in Kenya; scavenger.

**African Fish Eagle**
Medium-sized, striking chestnut brown and white colour; far-carrying melodious call a characteristic sound in bush; always near water, fisheater.

**Long-Crested Hawk Eagle**
Small, brown-black; very long crest; in savanna and farmland, often perched on telephone poles; hunts rats and mice.

**Martial Eagle**
Very large, brownish-grey upperparts, black throat, underparts white with dark spots; rounded crest; hunts game birds, monkeys, hyrax, small antelopes.

**Bateleur**
Very distinctive; broad, pointed wings, very short tail, nape crested; head and belly black, wing underside white, otherwise chestnut; "artistic" glider; feeds on small game, carrion in savanna and bush country.

**Augur Buzzard**
Most common bird of prey in all open areas of East Africa, often seen perched on telephone poles. Underparts white, upperparts dark grey, rufous tail.

**African Black Kite**
Brown, forked tail, yellow beak; common in all open areas, cultivated and settled areas; feeds on insects, birds, reptiles, carrion, refuse.

**Pale Chanting Goshawk**
Upright, pale grey, barred belly,

orange legs and base of bill; hunts birds and small mammals in bush and savanna; solitary.

## 8. Game birds

**Francolins**
About 10 different species, partridge-like; brown, some with yellow, orange or red at head and throat; family coveys, during breeding season in pairs; dry and moist savannas, bush.

**Helmeted Guinea-Fowl**
Bluish-black with white spots, bare blue neck and head, conspicuous bony helmet; in flocks, abundant in savanna, bush, cultivated land.

**Vulturine Guinea-Fowl**
Handsome, long-tailed, long-legged; cobalt-blue, spotted white; feathers of chest and upper mantle long and striped black-white-blue; small head and neck bare, blue; in flocks in acacia and semi-desert scrub of northeast Kenya.

## 9. Cranes, Bustards

**Crowned Crane**
Grey, wings black, white and brown; bare cheeks white and red; head with black velvet cap and tuft of straw-coloured, bristle-like feathers behind; loud call, usually in flight; in pairs; feeds on locusts, other insects, small animals, seeds, grain, etc.; in wetlands, open plains, cultivated areas.

**Kori Bustard**
Largest bustard species (100–130 cm), slim and long-legged; neck and upperparts greyish-brown, underparts white; dark crest on top of head; singly or in pairs; marvellous display from cock with throat pouch inflated and white ornamental feathers fluffed out; common in dry open plains and bush country.

## 10. Waders and Gulls

Muddy lake shores, swamps and moist savannas of East Africa teem with huge flocks of sandpipers and plovers, most of them migratory birds from Europe: wood sandpipers, green sandpipers, turnstones, ruffs, ringed plovers, greenshanks, avocets, stilts. Some typical resident African species:

**Crowned Plover**
Greyish-brown, white belly, black-and-white crown, red legs and bill.

**Blacksmith Plover**
Conspicuous; black, white and grey; loud, shrill "tik-tik-tik" call.

**Spurwing Plover**
Back greyish-brown, belly and crested crown black, neck white, small spur on bend of wing.

**Wattled Plover**
Pale olive-brown, white forehead and abdomen; red and yellow wattle in front of eye; yellow legs.

**Grey-Headed Gull**
Medium-sized; pale grey and white, distinctive grey head, red bill and legs.

**African Skimmer**
Upperparts black, underparts white, very long wings, scissor-like red bill flattened laterally. With its elongated lower mandible it catches small fish by skimming along and ploughing surface of water, usually at dusk.

## 11. Doves and Pigeons

**Speckled Pigeon**
Size of domestic pigeon; chestnut back, white spotted wings, otherwise blue-grey; eyes ringed red; common in savanna, on rocky hillsides, in cultivated areas; many breed in human habitations.

**Red-Eyed Dove**
Brownish-grey with black collar; common in wooded areas, gardens and human settlements.

**Namaqua Dove**
Sparrow-sized, very long tail, male bird has black on face and throat; common in thornbush and semi-desert.

## 12. Turacos and Cuckoos

**Hartlaub's Turaco**
Most common of six species found in East Africa; arboreal, in highland forests. Neck and underparts green; upperparts, tail and crown bluish-black; crimson flight feathers (very conspicuous in flight); bare red and white around eye.

**White-Bellied Go-Away-Bird**
Magpie-sized, grey, black and white, long tail, crest; arboreal, in dry bush and savanna; penetrating call "gaarr-waarr" (rendered as "go awayaaa" – hence the common name).

**White-Browed Coucal**
Magpie-sized, clumsy-looking; upperparts chestnut, underparts light brown, head and neck striped black-and-white, long black tail; in wooded and cultivated areas.

## 13. Owls

**Pearl-Spotted Owlet**
Little more than sparrow-sized; round head, no ear tufts; white spots on brown flight and tail feathers; in savanna and bush country; often diurnal; call "we-oo, we-oo".

**Spotted Eagle-Owl**
Medium-sized, thickset, tawny brown mottled greyish-white, round white spots on mantle, distinctive ear tufts.

**Verreaux's Eagle Owl**
Large, brownish-grey, finely marked, no spots; facial disc whitish with black band on each side and ear tufts; in savanna and bush, usually near water; sometimes seen sleeping by day in acacia tree-top.

## 14. Rollers, Kingfishers and Allies

Large group of very varied, usually colourful, long-billed birds.

**Lilac-Breasted Roller**
One of most beautiful East African birds; dove-sized, slender, long tail streamers; underparts and wing coverts ultramarine blue, upperparts brown, throat and breast lilac;

solitary, in savanna and bush; feeds on insects.

**Pied Kingfisher**
Black-and-white, long black bill, crested crown; singly on inland waters and at coast; hovers above water with rapidly beating wings, then drops headlong like a stone.

**Grey-Headed Kingfisher**
Head grey, breast and belly dark chestnut, upperparts black, wings and tail bright cobalt blue, red bill; singly in wooded areas near water, hunts fish, insects.

**Woodland Kingfisher**
Greenish-blue; black wing coverts, red bill and eyes, black feet; frequents savanna and open woodland near water, catches fish, insects.

**Pigmy Kingfisher**
Small, colourful (blue and chestnut, red bill); usually singly; feeds on fish fry (in reeds of waters) and insects (in savanna grass).

**Malachite Kingfisher**
Small; resembles pigmy kingfisher but crested crown; near water, feeds on small fish and dragonfly larva.

**Bee-Eaters**
Medium-sized, slim, brilliant plumage, long-tailed, wings tapered, bill slightly curved; insectivorous; lives in dry savanna, thornbush and semi-desert; sociable. Several species in East Africa.

**African Hoopoe**
Plumage bright rufous, wings and tail black barred white, high erectile crest, curved bill; insectivorous; lives in open areas; penetrating call.

**Green Wood Hoopoe**
Medium-sized, slender, long tail, red curved bill; black plumage, hints of green and purple, white on wings and tail; red feet; arboreal, gregarious; in savanna, parks.

**Red-Billed, Yellow-Billed Hornbills**
Medium-sized; upperparts brownish-black, white spotted wing coverts, underparts white; long tail; large, distinctive, curved bill; in dry bush and semi-desert; mainly insectivorous; female walled up in nest in tree hollow for 3 months, fed by male.

**Ground Hornbill**
Largest of African hornbills; usually seen in pairs on ground in grassland and savanna; feeds on insects, small reptiles, mammals; black with white flight feathers; bare face and throat bright red in males, red or blue in females; two species found in Kenya.

## 14. Songbirds

Nearly half of all bird species on earth are songbirds. The vast diversity of weavers, waxbills, starlings, warblers, thrushes, flycatchers, larks, longclaws, sunbirds, shrikes, swallows, swifts, crows, etc. found in East Africa is baffling for the amateur. To mention but a few examples:

**Dark-Capped Bulbul**
Common garden bird found throughout East Africa; greyish-brown upperparts, white belly, blackish hood; beautiful fluting song.

1. African Skimmer *(Rhynchops flavirostris)*; 2. Helmeted Guinea-Fowl *(Numida meleagris)*; 3. Bateleur *(Terathopius ecaudatus)*; 4. Ruppell's Vulture *(Gyps ruppellii)*; 5. Crowned Crane *(Balearica regulorum)*; 6. Pied Kingfisher *(Ceryle rudis)*; 7. Lilac-Breasted Roller *(Coracias caudata)*; 8. White-Bellied Go-Away-Bird *(Corythaixoides lencogaster)*; 9. White-Throated Bee-Eater *(Merops albicollis)*; 10. Paradise Flycatcher *(Tersiphone viridis)*; 11. Holub's Golden Weaver *(Ploceus xanthops)*; 12. Red-Billed Oxpecker *(Buphagus erythorynchus)*; 13. Abyssinian Ground Hornbill *(Bucorvus abyssinicus)*.

**Drongo**
Thrush-sized, plumage black, forked tail; widespread in savanna, bush, garden and cultivated areas; solitary, perches on telephone wires, trees, catches insects in flight, returns to same perch.

**Paradise Flycatcher**
Male has very long tail; head and breast black, otherwise chestnut and grey. In eastern Kenya (e. g. Tsavo) white plumage in males is more common than normal colour.

**Fiscal Shrike**
One of commonest and best-known East African birds, found everywhere, even in townships. Upperparts black and white, underparts white, tail long; usually seen singly, perched on bushes, telephone wires; insectivorous.

**Superb Starling**
Upperparts and breast glossy black, blue and green; chestnut belly; white band across breast; yellow eyes; sociable; common in thornbush savanna, often near human settlements, in hotel gardens, near lodges.

**Hildebrandt's Starling**
Similar to superb starling, but lacking white band across breast; eyes red; common in southern parts of Kenya.

**Splendid Glossy Starling**
Large; upperparts dark metallic blue and green, underparts glossy violet; eyes yellow; pairs or small flocks in savanna woodland from western Kenya to Uganda; fruit-eater.

**Rüppell's Long-Tailed Starling**
Dark metallic blue, violet and green, very long tail, whitish eyes; in savanna and bush country.

**Blue-Eared Glossy Starling**
Metallic green; yellow eyes; gregarious; common in all open areas and on cultivated land.

**Redwing Starling**
Large; glossy violet-black, rufous flight feathers distinctive in flight; red eyes; in rocky regions, wooded and cultivated areas, even in Nairobi City.

**Red-Billed Oxpecker**
Sociable; olive to brown in colour, thick red bill, yellow around eyes. In association with large game and domestic stock, feeding on ticks and ectoparasites in coat. Yellow-billed oxpecker similar, not found in eastern Kenya.

**Sunbirds**
Small birds with slender curved bills. Males metallic green, bronze or violet, some red or yellow at breast or belly, some with elongated central tail feathers. Females plain and hard to identify. Rapid, fluttering flight; usually in pairs; feed on nectar and insects.

Common species in East Africa: malachite sunbird (green), tacazze sunbird (violet), scarlet-chested sunbird (metallic green, scarlet breast), amethyst sunbird (velvety black, purple throat, green hood), variable sunbird (blue-green, violet chest patch, ochre belly).

**Weavers, Waxbills and Allies:** Largest bird family in Africa; most are seed-eaters with short heavy bills; sociable, nesting in colonies; true weavers build very elaborate nests of grass and other fibres. Notable species:

**White-Headed Buffalo Weaver,** large; head, neck and underparts white, upperparts brown with striking orange-red rump and under tail coverts; black bill; parrot-like appearance; dry acacia wood land.

Following are mainly yellow: **golden weaver** (orange throat), **black-headed weaver, Speke's weaver** and **masked weaver. Reichenow's weaver** has black upperparts and sides of face.

Small waxbills are often found together with starlings at bird feeding places in lodges. **African fire finch** is purple with white spotted breast; **cut-throat** greyish-brown with crimson band at throat; **waxbill** greyish-brown with red streak at eye; **red-cheeked cordon-bleu** greyish-brown above, underparts and tail blue, red cheek patch.

**Paradise Whydah**
Male in breeding season grows long, tapered tail feathers, up to twice body length; impressive courtship display; mainly black, neck and belly yellow, chestnut breast; female plain greyish-brown. Eggs laid in nest of green-winged pytilia, a waxbill. In grasslands and bush country.

**Pin-Tailed Whydah**
Males in breeding season grow long slender black tail double body length; head and upperparts black, underparts white, red bill; female plain brown. Eggs laid in nest of waxbill. In courtship display male hovers, "dancing" in the air over the female perched below. Common on grassland and pastureland.

**Pied Crow**
Black crow with white breast and white collar on neck. Sociable; common in all open areas, also near human habitations.

**Cape Rook**
Glossy black with slender bill; on open plains, cultivated land.

**Indian House Crow**
Glossy black with a strong bill. Introduced to Zanzibar from India 100 years ago, now also common on mainland (especially Mombasa and Nairobi).

## Reptiles

**Snakes**
Only exceptionally do tourists come across a snake in East Africa. Fear is unnecessary, but caution advisable. Sometimes a **black mamba** may be seen by roadside, largest poisonous snake in Africa (up to 4 m, slender, grey-brown); rarely smaller **green mamba** in acacia; both are arboreal and shy. Plump, sluggish **puff adder** is about 1.5 m long, brownish with zigzag pattern on back, hides in steppe grass, but common everywhere. **Rock python** is

non-venomous, up to 7 m long, lives among rocks, in dry areas.

**Nile Crocodile**
Up to 7 m long; once found at most lakes and rivers; now endangered by excessive hunting and poaching. Diet: Animal carcasses; mammals (up to buffalo-size) going to drink are pulled under water and drowned, lacerated, eaten when putrefied. In some waters (e. g. Lake Turkana, Lake Baringo) crocodiles feed almost solely on fish.

**Nile Monitor**
Up to 2 m long; yellowish bands and spots on dark green. Always near water; excellent swimmer and diver. Diet: Amphibians, fish, snails, mussels, crocodile and bird eggs.

**Common Agama**
Long-tailed, slender lizard (total length about 40 cm); basks in sun on rocks, walls, etc. in dry regions; orange head, otherwise bluish-green to black; changes colour (temperature, behaviour pattern); diurnal, insectivorous.

**Chameleons**
Medium-sized, green or brown lizards (they change colour!); in trees and bushes; two digits of feet as gripping device; prehensile tail and long tongue (catching insects). In East Africa: **Jackson's chameleon** (three horns on forehead, pointing forwards) and **double-banded chameleon,** both ovoviviparous (12–25 young).

**Geckos**
Small, nocturnal lizards; adhesive pads on digits mean they can run along vertical surfaces, even on ceilings, searching for insects. Grey-green **tropical gecko** is commonest species in East Africa, now also found in Latin America.

**Land Tortoises**
**Leopard tortoise** found in highland savannas; body length up to 65 cm, dark brown patches on yellow; does not feed during dry season. **African spurred tortoise** similarly frugal, but larger (up to 75 cm), yellow, flat-backed, heavily ridged shell; lives in dry savannas and semi-deserts.

# "Hatari!" Animal Paradises in Danger

With the exploration, colonization and development of East Africa at the beginning of this century, the rapid downfall of nature began. Nowhere has man shown his madness more clearly than in the destruction of the marvelously rich animal life in the East African grasslands. Unscrupulous big game hunts in the early colonial period, slayings en masse in World War II to feed prisoners of war, and a completely nonsensical extermination campaign lasting decades (using troops, all kinds of hoofed animals were slaughtered in an attempt to combat the tsetse fly) have meant that East Africa's fauna has been reduced to barely a fifth of its original size.

However, the greatest danger to nature is posed – as everywhere on our planet – by the rapidly increasing claims on, and destruction of, natural landscapes as a result of man's needs.

With an annual population growth rate of almost 4%, i. e. a doubling of the population in 20 years, Kenya is the fastest growing African nation. Some 87% of Kenya's 18 million inhabitants are country-dwellers, tilling the land and keeping cattle. Since 80% of the country's area is unsuitable for agriculture except at subsistence level, most of the population engaging in agriculture is concentrated on the remaining 20%. The growth in the population has meant, however, that more and more land (including the poorest of soils) has been claimed for agricultural purposes. Thanks to improved veterinary care, herds of cattle, sheep and goats are growing, a fact which has meant ever greater competition for grazing in the East African grasslands between domestic and wild animals. Domestic animals, unaccustomed as they are to the natural grazing conditions of Africa, are choosier than zebras and antelopes. They leave hard, thick-stemmed grasses well alone, therefore worsening the condition of pasturelands as a result of uneven use and trampling of the grass by large herds. More than a quarter of Kenya's approximately 20 million cattle, sheep and goats are barely able to survive today on "range land". When no rain falls – which is often the case for years in parts of Africa – catastrophe looms. In desperation, the cattle-keeping Masai drive their cattle, dying in their thousands of thirst, into the national parks, the last refuge of wild animals. (In 1976, they even reached the streets of Nairobi.)

The competition between domestic and wild animals – a losing battle for the latter in view of the ever-increasing demand for food (and therefore land) – has already led to Kenya's becoming almost devoid of wild animals outside the national parks and game reserves. A natural symbiosis of plants and animals in the thorn scrub and grasslands only exists in a few legally protected areas which are presented to tourists as the last animal paradises. However, not one of these protected areas would be able to survive as an ecological unit were it not for some form of human assistance. Only scientifically planned "Wildlife Management" will prevent Kenya's wildlife's dying out completely in the next few decades.

Such management will have to include utilization of the country's natural resources. Western ideals of man's moral responsibility to preserve nature have to be questioned in Africa in view of the other overwhelming problems which exist there. Western civilization, of such influence in the nineteenth and twentieth centuries, was responsible not only for "progress", but also for fateful developments in the Third World.

It is now up to the peoples of East Africa to learn to help themselves, to put the riches of nature to ecologically sensible use and at the same time to preserve them for future generations. Wild hoofed animals do no damage to plants and soil in an undisturbed biotope. They make optimum use of the food available, their water requirements are low, they are immune to most cattle diseases, and therefore produce, per square kilometre, more meat – and cheaper meat – than domestic animals. The care, protection and controlled exploitation of wild animals in East Africa could do a great deal towards solving the problem of feeding the indigenous population (as they already have in South Africa).

At the same time such measures could contribute to the preservation of nature. Another factor which should not be overlooked is the income from official, government-organized sales of skins, trophies and ivory. This would also make poaching – so far practically impossible to stem – superfluous. Soil conservation programmes and the use of solar energy for domestic requirements could put a halt to the widespread destruction of Africa's forests as a result of tree clearance to gain land, and tree-felling for firewood and charcoal.

International tourism too, which has become the most important source of income for the young countries of East Africa (in Kenya approximately US$ 100 million p. a.), can only be maintained by careful control of Africa's wildlife stock. The latter is concentrated to such an extent in the national parks and game reserves that the very existence of the natural habitat is endangered. Organizations such as the World Wildlife Fund (WWF) and the International Union for the Conservation of Nature and Natural Resources (IUCN) help to save what can be saved with financial contributions and specialist knowledge, and by lobbying government authorities and enlightening the population.

When in East Africa, support, through your own behaviour, the Kenyan government in its efforts to preserve nature. That poachers in

Kenya over the last ten years have killed half the elephants and almost 90% of the rhinoceros population are alarming figures and ones which should not be ignored.

When buying souvenirs, please remember that the export of ivory, skins, horns, turtle shells and other animal products is strictly prohibited. Kenya is one of the more than 90 member states of the Convention on International Trade in Endangered Species, the aim of which is to stop trade in threatened animal and plant species once and for all. Let's hope that the nicest memories of your trip to Kenya will be of stalking with your camera! *(Wünschmann)*

# National Parks and Game Reserves

As long ago as the end of the last century it became apparent that the decimation of East Africa's wild animals by man would eventually mean their end. In order to feed the indigenous human population, large areas of forest and huge herds were lost through tree clearance and game hunting. In addition, Arab tradesmen, Africans and Europeans had been hunting precious ivory and other trophies long before big game hunting became a popular sport. The situation became so grave that strict hunting laws were deemed absolutely necessary and introduced in German East Africa. And in British East Africa, again before the turn of the century, the first national park was created when the Athi plain, the area covered today by the Nairobi National Park, was made a game reserve. Further national parks were created before World War I to protect Kenya's flora and fauna.

There is a major difference between national parks and game reserves. The former serve to protect nature as a whole – landscape, plants and animals. The government permits the area to be developed touristically, which means that roads and lodges may be built where necessary. It also means that, to maintain an equilibrium, numbers of a particular species are controlled (as was the case when elephants were shot in Tsavo Park because it was feared that they would, with their huge food requirements, consume food needed by other animals).

Such measures would never be taken in game reserves since their principal function is the protection of animals. Farming on land which has been declared a game reserve is only allowed in isolated cases where tribes have long-established rights to the land.

Whether national park or game reserve, however, fauna and flora are protected, and visitors are sure to enjoy nature in all its richness.

A fee has to be paid to enter the national parks. In some reserves or parks visitors have to travel with a ranger. This can in fact be very useful as the ranger will know the terrain inside out. As some parks are closed during the rainy season, it is advisable to inquire beforehand about opening times.

More information on regulations to be observed in national parks and game reserves is given in the section "Rules on Safari".

### Wildlife Sanctuaries

**Aberdare National Park**
The park covers 770 sq. km (297 sq. miles) of mountainous land consisting of montane rainforest, heath and moorland, and bamboo forests. The most interesting animals here are elephants, lions and leopards, black rhinoceros, giant forest hogs, waterbucks and bushbucks, and spotted hyaenas. If luck is on your side you might also catch a glimpse of the rare bongo early in the morning. The forest hotels Treetops and The Ark are located in this park.

**Amboseli National Park**
See Masai Amboseli Game Reserve.

**East Turkana National Park**
The park, which covers 1,570 sq. km (606 sq. miles) on the eastern shore of Lake Turkana, was created specifically to protect the crocodiles living there.

**Kisite – Mpunguti Marine National Park**
A park consisting of four coral islands south of Shimoni (at the southeastern tip of the Kenya-Tanzania border). The coral gardens are considered to be the finest on Africa's east coast. The Pemba Channel Fishing Club provides simple but pleasant living quarters.

**Lake Nakuru National Park**
Lying in the Rift Valley, the park covers 202 sq. km (78 sq. miles) and encompasses Lake Nakuru and the surrounding reeds and marshlands. Lake Nakuru is known most of all as a bird paradise (up to 400 different species). The flamingos are particularly spectacular – depending on the water level (the lake is fed by the Njoro river) up to 2 million flamingos can be seen on and around the lake at any one time. In addition, there are hippos, lions, buffalos, waterbucks and giraffes in the park.

Accommodation: Lion Hill Camp and Lake Nakuru Lodge.

**Malindi Marine Park**
The marine park consists of Malindi Marine National Park (10,5 sq. km/ 4 sq. miles) and Watamu Marine National Park (5 sq. km/2 sq. miles) and is an area in which the marvellous coral of the coast is protected. At low tide the coral gardens can be admired on foot; otherwise, tours in glass-bottomed boats are available. Regulations regarding coral and shells are strict (it is forbidden to collect either) and the park authorities are keen to see that these regulations are observed.

**Marsabit National Park**
Situated on the mountain of the same name in northern Kenya, the park is 592 sq. km (228 sq. miles) in size and lies within the 2,000 sq. km (772 sq. miles) Marsabit Game Reserve. Mt. Marsabit is clothed in

cloud forest and woodland; the surrounding savanna and semi-desert regions are home to elephants, lions, leopards and rhinoceros, Grévy's zebras, greater kudus, bushbucks, gerenuks and Grant's gazelles.

Accommodation: Marsabit Lodge and Marsabit Tented Lodge.

**Meru National Park**

Situated northeast of Mount Kenya, the park covers 820 sq. km (316 sq. miles) and consists of broad grass plains, bush, acacia woodlands and dense forests along watercourses. Among the big game to be sighted in the park are elephants, lions, leopards, cheetahs, black and white rhinoceros, hippos (on the Tana River, the park's southern boundary), reticulated giraffes and gerenuks, lesser kudus, Grévy's and other zebras.

Accommodation: Meru Mulira Lodge and Leopard Rock Safari Lodge.

**Mount Elgon National Park**

An isolated, unspoilt park covering 170 sq. km (66 sq. miles) and situated near the Uganda border. In this area of montane forest and bamboo jungle, animals are more elusive. Huge caves within the park were once inhabited by the Elgon Masai; nowadays only bats and watering animals are to be found.

Accommodation: Mount Elgon Lodge.

**Mount Kenya National Park**

The 770 sq. km (297 sq. mile) park lies approx. 210 km (130 miles) north of Nairobi. The three peaks of Mt. Kenya (Batian at 5,199 m, Nelion at 5,188 m, and Lanana at 4,985 m) tower above the park. Weather conditions permitting, any fairly fit person can climb Lalana. Below snow-capped peaks and glaciers, moorlands with giant lobelias and groundsel are characteristic of Mt. Kenya. Below these moorlands the park abounds in elephants, leopards, black rhinoceros, forest hogs, bushbucks, buffalos and many species of birds.

Accommodation: Mountain Lodge, Naro Moru River Lodge, or the luxurious Mount Kenya Safari Club.

**Nairobi National Park**

The park covers some 120 sq. km (46 sq. miles) and lies just a few kilometres from Nairobi. Grassy plains predominate but there are also wooded areas. At the main gate to the park the Nairobi Animal Orphanage cares for young and injured animals. Although the park is small and so near the city, a visit is definitely worthwhile to see lions, leopards, cheetahs, baboons, green monkeys, black rhinoceros, zebras, warthogs, hippopotamuses, antelopes, dik-diks, waterbucks, mountain bucks, Thomson's and Grant's gazelles, impalas, elands and Masai giraffes.

Accommodation: Masai Lodge.

**Ol Doinyo Sapuk National Park**

Situated southeast of Thika, the park covers 20 sq. km (8 sq. miles). A great many buffalo and impala live in the park. The Fourteen Falls are not very far away and are well worth a visit.

**Olorgesailie National Park**
Lying in the Rift Valley between Nairobi and Lake Magadi, the park covers 4 sq. km (1½ sq. mile). An important archaeological excavation site, the Leakeys made important prehistoric finds in the area in 1942. A great variety of birds can be seen in the park. Larger game include gerenuks, klipspringers and rhinoceros.

**Tsavo National Park**
Kenya's biggest national park, Tsavo is 20,800 sq. km (8,000 sq. miles) in size. It is split into Tsavo East and Tsavo West by the road from Mombasa to Nairobi.

Tsavo East consists of flat dry scrub and grassland. Lugard's Falls on the Galana river are spectacular. Numerous animals can be observed in the park: elephants and lions, leopards and cheetahs, crocodiles, hyaenas, Masai giraffes and black rhinoceroses, hippopotamuses and zebras, hartebeests and gerenuks, lesser kudus and elands, impalas and klipspringers, waterbucks and Grant's and Thomson's gazelles.

Accommodation: Voi Safari Lodge.

Tsavo West is partly mountainous and partly covered by savanna and grassland. Black lava streams and the Mzima Springs are especially interesting phenomena.

Accommodation: Kilaguni Lodge, Ngulia Lodge, Taita Hills and Salt Lick Lodge.

It is worth bearing in mind that the Tsavo National Park is not far from the coast (and holiday hotels there) and that Tsavo often features on extended safaris. It is therefore advisable to book accommodation well in advance.

**Watamu Marine National Park**
See Malindi Marine Park.

## Game Reserves

**Arawale Game Reserve**
Located on the left bank of the Tana river; created for the protection of hartebeests.

**Bisinadi Reserve**
Borders on Meru National Park and is similarly stocked.

**Boni Reserve**
On the Somalian border, north of the Kiunga road. The reserve was created to protect the elephants living there.

**Crescent Island Reserve**
Small island (1.5 sq. km/½ sq. mile) in Lake Naivasha; home to more than 340 bird species.

**Dodoni Reserve**
South of the Kiunga road (See Boni Reserve).

**Kora Reserve**
Located on the southern bank of the Tana river.

**Lake Bogoria Reserve**
In the East African Rift Valley, created to protect the fauna and flora of the salt lake; hot springs, a geysir and a profusion of bird life.

# Rules on Safari

For anyone who would like to observe and photograph wild animals in the expanses of the national parks but is not an experienced bushman, the ideal solution is probably an organized safari. Minibuses which are specially equipped for difficult terrain and other cross-country vehicles are driven by experienced guides. The guides (who act as driver, guide, scout and trailseeker) are always very familiar with a particular area and will explain everything to visitors, usually in English. They know the shady spots where lions doze in the midday sun, the trees on which the elusive leopard consumes its prey from the night before, the places where the big herds gather at a particular time of year, always on the move in search of waters and new grazing. And they know how close one can safely get to Africa's grey giants, the majestic elephants.

But for those who really seek adventure and would like to get to know Kenya off their own bat by planning an independent safari through the game reserves and national parks, a few things should be kept in mind. Besides strict regulations governing visits to the parks, there are certain basic rules which Kenyans and regular visitors to Kenya take pains to uphold.

As far as planning your itinerary goes, it's usually recommended that those going it alone spend two to three days on the wide plains of the Tsavo National Park and the Amboseli and Mara Reserves, a further two days in the highlands, and around three days in the north and in the mountains. This would be just enough time to get to know Kenya. Self-drive cars as well as cars with driver can be rented for such trips. The advantage of having a driver – besides the freedom this allows you while on the road – lies in the explanations and tips which most safari drivers are able to give regarding terrain and wildlife. But whether you are travelling with a driver or on your own, the following guidelines should be observed:

- In Kenya traffic drives on the left.
- A good road map, tools, a spare wheel and a reserve can of petrol belong in every car.
- Always enquire where the next filling station is.
- Animals have right of way in the national parks and game reserves.
- Only leave the car at the places provided.
- At sundown leave the park or put in at a lodge.
- Book accommodation at a lodge in advance as often all places will be booked.
- Camping is only allowed at the camps provided for this purpose.
- Don't light fires.

Safari lodges are a Kenyan invention. They enable visitors to sit in comfortable surroundings and still observe and photograph animals at close quarters when they come to waterholes to drink in the early morning and evening. As a rule, lodges outside the parks are less expensive than those within the park boundaries.

In the national parks north of Nairobi and in the mountains, the animals are wilder and more timid than elsewhere and it is therefore usual to head straight for a lodge on arrival. In the national parks in the south (Tsavo, Amboseli, Mara) it is possible to move around relatively freely. But farther northwards, where the highland plateau gives way to desert, it is easier to observe animals roaming free without being restricted to a particular base.

**Lambwe Valley Reserve**
Covers 260 sq. km (100 sq. miles), mainly grassland but with several wooded tracts; large numbers of roan antelope and buffalo can be found.

**Maralal Reserve**
In the Rift Valley between Nairobi and Lake Turkana on the Lerogi Plateau.

**Masai Amboseli Game Reserve**
The 3,200 sq. km (1,235 sq. miles) of the reserve encompasses 380 sq. km (146 sq. miles) which were declared a national park in 1974. One of Kenya's largest and best-loved reserves. Kilimanjaro, at 5,895 m Africa's highest mountain, forms an impressive backdrop to the reserve.

In the scrub and acacia forests of the park, and especially near the swamps, one can see elephants and lions, leopards and cheetahs, various jackals and zebras, black rhinoceros and warthogs, hippopotamuses and buffalos, hartebeests and gnus, waterbucks and impalas, Thomson's and Grant's gazelles, gerenuks, giraffes and lesser kudus, as well as a great many different species of bird.

**Masai Mara Reserve**
Some 512 sq. km (197 sq. miles) of the total area of 1,792 sq. km (692 sq. miles) have been declared a national park. Masai Mara borders on Tanzania's Serengeti National Park, and fauna, flora and landforms blend with those of the Serengeti. An abundance of wildlife is to be found here on hilly savannas, rolling grasslands, and in the gallery forests along the Mara and its tributaries. Apart from huge herds of plains game, there are many lions and topis, crocodiles in the Mara river, hippos in so-called hippo pools. Larger species of bird include guinea fowl, bustards and secretary birds.

Accommodation: Keekorok Lodge, Mara Serena Lodge, Kichwa Tembo Camp, Governor's Camp, Mara Buffalo Camp, Mara Cottar's

Camp, Mara Sara Camp, Mara River Camp.

**Ngong National Reserve**
Situated in the Ngong Hills southwest of Nairobi. The 320 sq. km (123 sq. miles) of the reserve border on the Nairobi National Park. The animal stock is similar to that found in the Nairobi Park, the herds having access to both.

**Rahole National Reserve**
Rahole lies opposite the Kora National Reserve on the Tana River just east of Meru National Park.

**Saiwa Swamp National Reserve**
Located northwest of Kitale near the Ugandan border and the Mount Elgon National Park. Made into a reserve in 1972 for the protection of the rare sitatunga or marshbuck (an antelope with wide hooves adapted to marshy ground).

**Shimba Hills National Reserve**
Located southwest of Mombasa, the reserve occupies some 190 sq. km (72 sq. miles) of hilly country at the Indian Ocean coast. A picturesque landscape and an abundance of wildlife make Shimba Hills an ideal destination for anyone based in Mombasa interested in a short safari. The rare sable antilope – introduced only a few years ago but now well-established – is a special attraction.

**Samburu/Isiolo/Shaba Game Reserves**
Three reserves covering an area of 300 sq. km (116 sq. miles) on both banks of the Uaso Nyiro River north of Mount Kenya. Fairly dense vegetation along the river; otherwise dry savanna and scrub. The waters of the river have made for an abundance of wildlife. The reticulated giraffe, Grevy's zebra and the beisa oryx are peculiar to the region.

**Tana River Primate Reserve**
One of Kenya's newer reserves, created to protect primates. Situated on the Tana River inland from Lamu island. Riverine vegetation makes for good conditions for animal life.

**West Chyulu National Reserve**
Borders on Tsavo National Park. In the wooded, volcanic Chyulu Hills.

## National Monuments

**Gedi Ruins/National Monument**
Ruins of an Arabian settlement in the midst of dense coastal forest just south of Malindi. Guided tours are available. Thought to have been established in the 14th century and abandoned in the 16th, excavations point to a thriving trading community. The course of events leading to the abandonment of the Arab town remains a mystery. (See also A–Z.)

**Jumba la Mtwana**
Ruins of a slave trading post on the Indian Ocean north of Mombasa. (See also A–Z.)

**Kariandusi**
Prehistoric site between Nakuru and Gilgil northwest of Nairobi. Excavation work carried out by the Leakeys from 1946 to 1947. *(Nenzel)*

# Diving and Underwater World

Although East Africa is thought of primarily as *the* place for safaris, it would be an unforgivable omission if one did not devote some space to the coral reefs which lie off the coast. Coral reefs can only exist in warm waters but conditions for their existence are not always the same, and forms of reef vary. For example, the reefs which stretch along the East African coast, and in particular along the coastlines of Kenya and Tanzania, are broad fringing reefs extending from the shore. They are found as far south as Mozambique but are scarce north of the equator, along the coast of Somalia, where cool ocean waters welling up from the deep preclude their presence.

At only a few spots along the Kenyan coast do the fringing reefs start directly at the shore. More often they are between 500 metres and 1.5 kilometres farther out. The lagoon between reef and shore is then characterized by expanses of sand and dead coral formations.

Generally speaking, the kinds of coral found off the East African coast are similar to those in other parts of the Indian and Pacific Oceans, but the appearance of the reefs is peculiar to East Africa. The main reason for this is the fact that water levels at high tide and low tide can vary by as much as 3–4 metres. Such a change in water level causes strong currents and continuously dredges up sand from the ocean bed. In addition, the steady "rain" of sediment which is carried over the reef when the tide ebbs from the lagoon means that many coral species cannot develop freely. As a result, only a few typical reef structures are found. Off the East African coast the reefs are flat and saddle-shaped, rising gently from depths of about only 20 m. In contrast, in the Red Sea – to take a not too far removed example – there are reefs with much steeper drop-offs. Numerous soft coral species, being resistant to the sediment raining down on them, are characteristic of the East African reefs.

The waters along the East African coast abound in plankton. At times, masses of these tiny organisms are swept along by the current, looking like clouds as they drift past. This affects visibility underwater, of course, and is particularly problematic during the rainy season and whenever a heavy sea churns up the ocean bed. At such times visibility may be reduced to 5 metres. Usually, however, visibility is much better – 10 to 15 metres – and on good days may even be as much as 20 to 25 metres.

Underwater photographers simply have to take appropriate measures to suit conditions and, when visibility is poor, concentrate on close-up pictures. However, by using extremely short focal length lenses (a 15 mm lens on the Nikonos, for example; otherwise, wide-angle or even fish-eye lenses built into the underwater camera housing) it is relatively easy to capture an overall impression of East Africa's underwater world instead of being limited to photographs of single fishes or frame-filling shots of other sea creatures.

The abundance of plankton does have definite advantages, too. Shots taken into the light source often capture a special mood, and the presence of these drifting feeding grounds guarantees pictures of underwater life at all stages of development. For it is not only the reef as such that lives from the plankton – besides myriads of coral polyps stretching out their tentacles, we find many other lower forms of life (for example, sponges or particularly enchanting crinoids) drawing nourishment from it, and for fish it is the basis of the food chain.

Many reefs support an incredible amount of animal life; there is not only an abundance of species, but also an immense variety of individuals. Most types of fish encountered here can in fact be seen at other diving spots in the Indian Ocean, but there are also numerous species which are typically African and are to be found here and nowhere else. Almost all of the fish are brightly coloured. There are coral fish about the size of a man's finger, somewhat larger butterfly and emporer fish and hussars, not forgetting surgeonfish, which look like jewels as they dart through the water.

Myriads of only centimetre-long, almost transparent glassfish can often be seen in front of cave entrances. Bizarre-looking, poisonous lion fish are encountered in predominantly shady places, and morays – real "shady characters" – vent their anger on unwelcome visitors from narrow crevices. Small striped clown fish snuggle down and feel at home in the tentacle forests of large sea anemones. Slim yellow trumpet fish, boxfish which are graceful yet at the same time droll, and innumerable other species are also found here. It is just impossible to list all the fish species in East African waters.

In addition, there are great varieties of crabs, shellfish and snails, echinoderms and sponges, and other sea creatures. On the outer edges of the coral reefs shoals of snappers scurry about. Jacks, too, are frequently to be seen and sometimes small groups of tuna appear. Big, tame morays can be hand-fed, and finally, giant groupers (which have been known to grow to the size of a small car) are also a familiar sight in the East African reefs. And everything that can be counted on to quicken a diver's pulse – including sharks – is there in the outer reefs.

With a bit of luck, it is even possible, further out, to encounter out-and-out giants: mantas, giant rays whose pectoral fins have a span of up to 5 metres, and whale sharks which are usually loners and have been known to grow up to 18 m in length. (The whale shark is in fact the largest known fish.) There is, however, no need to be afraid of either whale shark or manta as both are gentle giants. They have eliminated the intermediate members of the food chain and feed on plankton which they filter from the water with their huge mouths. Here, in the waters off the East African coast, they must think they are in a "sea of milk and honey"! As they are surface fish, they can be approached even better snorkelling than using an aqualung, and with a bit of luck and skill it is even possible to swing up onto their backs for a little joy-ride!

Fortunately, the Kenyan government is devoting just as much attention to nature underwater as on land. In order to protect the wonders of the deep, spear fishing is forbidden, coralls may not be exported, and a number of reefs have been made into nature reserves. In the north there's the Kiunga Marine Park, in the central coastal section, the Malindi Marine Park and the Watamu Marine National Park, and farther south, the Kisite/Mpunguti Marine National Park. In these areas it is an offence to collect shells, corals, etc. as souvenirs.

Of course, such regulations should serve as general guidelines in non-protected areas, too, For, whenever snorkellers and divers go into the sea, even seemingly harmless pleasures such as collecting shells and snails or removing starfish have far-reaching negative ecological consequences, as they are thus repeated thousands of times. Buying souvenirs in shops or from pedlars on the beach has an even more serious effect, because the reefs are then exploited specifically for economic gain.

Many people have a quite definite reason for deciding in favour of Kenya for a diving holiday. Not only is there the possibility of combining safari and diving, and therefore enjoying a unique vacation, but in addition, the friendly Kenyan people, their picture-book beaches, and the possibilities for amusement afforded by the latter mean that Kenya is an ideal destination, especially for those diving enthusiasts whose partners or travelling companions have not (yet) caught the diving bug!

To cast a first glance under the surface of the water, it is not necessary to stick to those spots where the reefs reach right up to the shore. Visitors can also take advantage of organized boat trips to areas which are ideal for snorkelling. Even those who do no more than participate in such a trip can be sure to experience a great many wonderful sights. (While doing so, however, keep in mind that it can be dangerous to underestimate the strength of the African sun. A fairly long cotton T-shirt gives good protection while still being light and cool.)

However, you only become a fish among fish when your time underwater is not limited to the short moments you can hold your breath for. For those wanting to dive using breathing gear, a diving base is essential, and not just for equipment hire and compressed air. The diving instructors who work in the various centres know all the nooks and crannies of the area they dive in. Every day they head for one of many very interesting spots (most are between half an hour and an hour away by boat) and then accompany their guests into the underwater world.

More experienced divers will bring most of their equipment with them: mask, flippers and snorkel, diving suit, life-jacket and safety instruments (depth gauge, etc.), and of course their own underwater film or photo equipment. They then only need hire the heaviest items – air tanks and weight belt.

Many diving bases require a doctor's certificate attesting fitness for diving. You should also take along your diving certificate and logbook to give an indication of the degree of experience you already have. Should you forget either certificate or logbook, the standard you have reached will be established by means of a test.

Inexperienced divers can book diving courses, borrow all the equipment they need, and take a test at the end of their course; the certificates which are awarded to successful participants are recognized all over the world.

A number of diving bases have been opened along the Kenyan coast in an area extending from south of Mombasa to north of Malindi. Most of these have links with international diving organizations, which in turn have a great deal of experience in the field of diving and diving holidays. The following is a list of the most important diving bases in Kenya.

Scuba Diving Kenya Ltd., which cooperates with the Poseidon-Nemrod Club, has its base in Turtle Bay, about 18 km (11 miles) south of Malindi. The base is open throughout the year. As well as daily diving trips, activities on offer at this base include training courses for beginners, windsurfing, deep-sea fishing and water-skiing, and trips in glass-bottomed boats and dhows. Underwater lamps, and underwater photo and film cameras can be rented. An underwater scooter is also available.

The Companie International Diving Schools also have a base in Turtle Bay, but this is only open from September to April. Training courses for beginners are available in addition to daily diving trips. It is also possible to go windsurfing and sailing, and to borrow underwater cameras.

The Barakuda Club Severin Sea Lodge, about 12 km (7½ miles) north of Mombasa, is open all the year round. As well as the usual diving trips, there are training courses for beginners; one and two star diving certificates (recognized worldwide) can be obtained here; windsurfing courses are also available. Underwater film and photo equipment may be hired here.

The Barakuda Club Diani Diving & Safaris is open throughout the year with the exception of May and June. Apart from the daily diving trips there are training courses for beginners; one star diving certificate tests can be taken here; and there are facilities for windsurfing and catamaran sailing. Underwater cameras can be rented, and there is also a photo laboratory.

In the Robinson Club Baobab, diving is also handled by the Barakuda Club. The club is closed in May and June. During the rest of the year, diving trips, training courses for beginners, one star diving certificate tests, windsurfing courses, deep-sea fishing and glass-bottomed boat trips are available.

The African Safari Club operates a diving base at the Mariani Club Hotel on Kilifi Creek. The base is open all year round. In addition to daily diving trips, there are training courses for beginners, windsurfing, mini-sailing, water-skiing, and yacht and boat day-trips to the best bathing beaches.

The best time of the year for diving is from October to the end of March. Although weather conditions are by no means always the same or particularly stable at this time of year, this period does encompass the best months of all (November to the beginning of December, and February/March), when waters are calm and visibility is at its best.

Diving can still be very good in April if the southeast monsoon has not started; if it has, however, freshening winds, heavy seas and rain restrict diving possibilities considerably. May and June in particular are extremely unfavourable for boat trips; July and August are better suited, but conditions can still be changeable and unreliable.

The extreme tidal differences have different effects in different places. This must obviously be borne in mind on diving trips. In many places trips can only be made at high tide (because of the reef passages), and diving around the clock is completely out of the question. However, diving at low tide is possible from Kilifi Creek as well as near Shimoni. Low tide usually affords the best visibility, by the way. Diving at both these spots is extremely fascinating, if for no other reason then because of the underwater caves. Otherwise, the most interesting places for diving are definitely those immediately in and around Turtle Bay and Watamu Beach; most of the spots here are part of the Marine National Park.

And finally, a few words on safety measures while diving. At all events follow the instructions given by your diving guide. This is of extreme importance, firstly because of the currents, which can be extremely unpleasant at times, and secondly, in order to avoid a decompression accident. However, the risk of such an accident happening is very low – the diving grounds are in relatively shallow water, and tropical coral reefs are at their most fascinating at such slight depths that, even after a fairly long stay beneath the surface, there is hardly ever any need to put in a decompression stop. You can indulge in "happy diving" here to your heart's content. However, this does not mean that you can afford to ignore dive tables. Rather, you should always check that you are really still within no-decompression limits. It's worth bearing in mind that none of the above-mentioned bases has a decompression chamber. The nearest is in Mombasa, which is about 80 km (50 miles) away from Turtle Bay, for instance. This is too far to make quick help possible in an emergency situation, even if transport by helicopter or small aircraft can be arranged.

*(Freihen)*

# The People of Kenya

The population of Kenya is made up of a great many different peoples. Altogether there are around 40 different ethnic groups, each with its own cultural, linguistic and physical characteristics. These different groups are usually classified according to the language they speak. Approximately 65% of the population speak a Bantu language, 30% a Nilotic language, and a minority 3% a Cushitic language. Bantu-speaking groups include the Kikuyu, Embu, Meru and Kamba of the interior, the Luyia and Gusii of Lake Victoria, and the Taita and Taveta of the southeast.

Nilotic groups include the Luo of Lake Victoria (the second-largest ethnic group after the Kikuyu), and the Turkana and Masai. The Turkana and Masai are pastoral nomads. The Somali people who live on the Kenya-Somalia border speak a Cushitic language. The language of the Swahili people along the coast has become the national language of Kenya. It can be seen as a hybrid language, since what is basically a Bantu language contains elements of Arabian (there was an Arab presence along the coast for well over five centuries) and European languages (the inevitable result of years of colonial rule).

The Kikuyu and the Luo are the two most important and influential groups in Kenya. The Kikuyu are a pastoralist people and live in the central highlands. The first European settlers made their homes in this fertile area, establishing their plantations on land which had traditionally belonged to the Kikuyu. The loss of this land meant that agriculture, the mainstay of the Kikuyu way of life, was threatened. They felt the effects of colonialism sooner and to a far greater extent than any other one group in Kenya, and therefore led opposition and resistance when it came. But it was also the Kikuyu who first benefitted from the educational advantages afforded by white settlement. This has meant that over the years they have always played a leading role in Kenyan politics and enjoyed a privileged position in Kenyan society. They were the driving force behind the Mau Mau rebellion in the fifties and it was a member of the Kikuyu – Jomo Kenyatta – who became first president of independent Kenya.

The Embu and Meru of Mount Kenya, people whose traditional dances are famous worldwide, are closely related to the Kikuyu.

For many years there was a great deal of animosity between the Kikuyu and the second-largest group of people in Kenya, the Luo. The main grievance of the Luo was that the Kikuyu had, and wished to retain, a privileged position in politics and commerce. Nowadays, however, prejudices are being broken down, and differences settled – particularly among the younger generation. Over a million Luo live in

Kenya today, for the most part in and around Kisumu. In many ways their way of life has changed to meet the demands of the twentieth century, but the Luo have managed to preserve their cultural heritage. Ceremonial dress, for example, which utilizes animal skins, teeth and bones is particularly impressive.

The Masai, a pastoralist group like the Turkana, have always been ready to fight for land, believing themselves to be the true lords of the savanna. This attitude inevitably led to conflict with the Kikuyu who had established settlements in savanna areas. The colonial authorities intervened in this continuing struggle for control of the land and, as a result of this, a section of the Masai settled and began to work the land as resident farmers.

Cultural and religious traditions are still an important part of the life of the Masai.

The "moran" system, for example, dates back to the time when all the Masai were nomadic pastoralists. Although nomadism has now become a thing of the past in most cases, the "moran" is still an important part of Masai life. Masai youths undergo initiation at the age of sixteen and are then ritually welcomed into the "moran", the warrior class of the Masai. The traditional role of the Masai warriors – that of guarding herds – is only rarely called upon today but the "moran" class has lost none of its importance. It represents one element of the structured order of life, the stages of which demand a great deal of self-discipline and self-negation from the Masai.

The Masai dress according to tradition. The men still wear a "shuka", a shoulder cloth coloured with red ochre pigment, and still carry spear and knife as well as bow and arrow. For the most part, they reject European clothing. Masai women still wear their traditional wide, beaded bands around the neck. Beaded earrings continue to be common among the men. The tall, slender Masai colour their hair with ochre and then style it elaborately.

Centuries ago the Samburu broke away from the Masai. Like the Turkana, they now live as pastoralists in the thornbush savanna north of Lake Turkana. Their whole existence centres around their livestock; with their animals they wander the land in search of fresh grazing.

The Somali of northeast Kenya are another pastoral group. They are found over an area which extends beyond Kenya's borders into Somalia and Ethiopia.

The Kenyan government is trying to unite the many different people who make up the population under the motto "Harambee" which calls on all Kenyans to come together and work together for the future. In this way it is hoped that conflicts like that between the Kikuyu and Luo will come to an end once and for all.

Europeans, Arabs and Asians (mainly Indians and Pakistanis) make up a minority of the Kenyan population. During the years of colonial rule the Asian community excelled in the field of commerce, creating what amounted to a monopoly. To a certain extent the same is true today, although the Kenyan government made a concerted attempt to change the situation in the seventies when many Asians who did not have Kenyan citizenship were expelled. At the present time there are approximately 80,000 Indians, 27,000 Arabs and 25,000 Europeans living in Kenya.

Approximately 20% of the Kenyan population belong to the Catholic church; 30% are Protestants. Estimates of the size of the Moslem community vary but it is generally thought that this accounts for approximately 5% of the population. For many Kenyans animism is still the main religious force in their lives; among rural groups, community life and the structure of society continue to be dictated by traditional beliefs.

The religious beliefs of the different ethnic groups in Kenya are most clearly expressed in their rituals and dances. It is a sad consequence of the growth of the tourist industry that such rituals and dances are so often "packaged" for foreign visitors, something which inevitably undermines their true meaning.

## A Few Words of Swahili

In Kenya, the language of trade and ordinary communication is English, and so you should have no difficulty making yourself understood there. The country's official language, Swahili, is a Bantu language with many borrowed words, initially from Arabic and then from English. Tourists would do well to learn a few words of Swahili, not just as an expression of courtesy but also because in some areas (for example, along the coast) English is by no means widely-spoken.

And it is always looked kindly upon when foreign tourists make an effort to speak to the native population in their own language. Most important of all is greeting someone, and there are definite forms of greeting which should be observed. If someone greets you with "Jambo" (Hello, Good morning), you should reply with "Jambo". If this is followed up by the question "Habari?" (How are you?), you should reply with "Mzuri" or "Njema". Both mean "I'm fine, thank you" – the Kenyans do not find it polite to say otherwise. If, having mastered the greeting, you feel you might try your hand at some other simple statements, the following list of words may be helpful:

Thank you – Ahsante sana
Please – Tafadhali
Bring me – Lete
I would like – Nataka, napenda
Now   Sasa
Quickly – Upesi, haraka
Today – Leo
Tomorrow – Kesho
Food – Chakula
Beer – Tembo
Coffee – Kahawa

Tea – Chai
Water – Maji
Milk – Maziwa
Bread – Mkate
Meat – Nyama
Fish – Samaki
Fruit – Matunda
Butter – Siagi
Sugar – Sukari
Salt – Chumvi
Warm – Moto
Cold – Baridi
A lot of – Mingi
Big – Mkubwa
Small, a little – Kidogo
Welcome – Karibu
Yes – Ndio
No – Hapana
I, me – Mimi
You, you – Wewe
And – Na
Here – Hapa
Later – Bado
How much (many)? – Ngapi?
One – Moja
Two – Mbili
Three – Tatu
Four – Nne
Five – Tano
Six – Sita
Seven – Saba
Eight – Nane
Nine – Tisa
Ten – Kumi
Eleven etc. – Kumi na moja etc.
Twenty – Ishirini
Twenty-one – Ishirini na moja
Where is? Where are? – Wapi...?
Where is (are)...? – Wapi...?
- a good hotel? – Hoteli mzuri?
- the toilet? – Choo
- the nearest doctor? – Daktari karibu
- a telephone? – Simu
- a filling station? – Garage
- a garage? – Fundi
- a chemist's? – Duka la dawa
- the main road? – Barabara

Slow – Pole-pole
I can't understand – Sifahamu
Left – Kushoto
Right – Kulia
Straight on – Moja kwa moja
Watch out! – Angalia!
Goodbye – Kwaheri

*(Nenzel)*

# The Culture of Kenya

Ethnography is that branch of anthropology which deals with the social forms and cultures of individual peoples. Such a study of East Africa is made difficult by a culture which is both multifarious and fragmented. That the population is continuing to change rapidly and extensively at the present time constitutes another difficulty. The end result is that any kind of ethnographic consideration of East Africa inevitably resorts to generalizations and to comparisons with neighbouring African societies.

The division of the African continent into the countries we know today was the outcome of European colonization in the late 19th and early 20th centuries. It is therefore a relatively recent event in the long history of the African people. The extraordinary mixture of racial and linguistic groups in Africa (each with its own political, economic, and cultural characteristics) came about as a result of adaptation to a particular environment over many years; it was not a result of the creation of boundaries during eighty years of colonial rule. This link with the physical environment is the basis of East Africa's great social and cultural diversity – a diversity which reflects clearly defined geographic and climatic zones.

The elevated area which we now know as East Africa was, in the course of its history, traversed by a great many different peoples. However, in spite of the influences which these racial groups undoubtedly exercised on each other, the role of the environment in determining evolution cannot be ignored. Pastoral peoples on the northern and eastern edges of Black Africa adapted in order to survive the extreme heat, developing a habitus which is particular to them: tall and slender, they are relatively light in body weight. In the same way, the small stature of the Pygmys is, to a large extent, the result of life in dense virgin forests. Even the various types of Negro which are found in Africa can be traced back to conditions prevalent at the edges of forests where they lived.

The importance of evolution can also be seen in an African's thinking, which tends to be cosmological and ancestor-oriented. In this he/she stands in sharp contrast to the Westerner, who expends far more of his/her thinking efforts in solving everyday practical problems by other means. Every African is deeply rooted in his past, and in East Africa this past goes right back to the origins of mankind. (It is quite interesting to note here that Africans believe that everything started with woman. Many Bantu tribes are matriarchies and the "tribal mother" is always honoured – even patriarchal Africans agree that "Man can only really be sure of the belly from which he was born".)

Just as evolution can be traced back many millions of years in East Africa, so too can the origins of East African culture be said to begin with Proconsul Africanus, a fossil ape thought to have been present in Kenya in the Miocene epoch approximately 25 million years ago. The development of culture later continues with Kenyapithecus (12 million years ago), with Homo habilis (2.5 million years ago), and finally with Homo sapiens, whose achievements mark the Middle Stone Age.

It was in fact in Kenya and neighbouring Tanzania that ancestors of modern man rose up on their hindlegs for the first time, thus liberating themselves from a purely quadrupedal existence. With their hands the hominids produced primitive tools with which they were able to master their environment. Many experts now believe that African hominids produced the first tools, and that the techniques they had developed spread in time to the other continents of the world. Some 15,000 years ago, therefore, primitive man in Africa and elsewhere was instrumental in a "discovery" which represented a turning point in history, and which resulted in ever greater differentiation of race and way of life. As a direct result of the development of tools, there soon existed contemporary African civilizations at varying stages of development.

The Capsian culture of Kenya, which emerged in the Upper Palaeolithic, developed autochthonous methods of manufacture which later merged with those of the Neolithic. The majority of tool finds show long, thin flakes chipped away from the centre of an obsidian. These new techniques made considerable advances in the manufacture of burins, scrapers, chisels, and other tools possible, thus enabling prehistoric man to fashion wood and bones. (The Capsian culture and the Elmenteitian culture which emerged from it were located in the east of the country. Bones found around Elmenteitia and Naivasha in Kenya show these people to have had long narrow skulls and faces.) Pre-Neolithic Capsians in eastern Africa and in the Sudan had already whetted stones into disc-shaped kernels. It is also certainly to the Capsians that we may attribute the development of pottery, a revolutionary step in human progress. The 5,000-year-old Elmenteitia pottery serves as evidence of the fact that knowledge of pottery, as well as of weapons and tools made of bones, reached the Sahara and Egypt from the East African highlands.

It is not easy to establish clear links between the different types of Homo sapiens who were present in East Africa in earlier times, and the tool users, evidence of whom was found by Dr. Leakey and his team of anthropologists. But it does seem likely that a dominant type, similar to the bushmen of today, gradually established itself, and was already to be found over most of the area by 1000 B. C. Certain cultures in Kenya can be traced back to the hunters and gatherers of the past. But, although for contemporary Africans genesis is ever-present, this is not to say that the Stone Age inhabitants of much of Kenya have survived as an ancient race. Boni, Sanye und Dorobo tribesmen are very much our contemporaries, but specific cultural aspects of an earlier age, as well as techniques dating from this time, have been preserved through them. It is therefore not a question of a blood relationship with Stone Age man, but of cultural continuity. Archaeological and linguistic research, as well as certain oral traditions, indicate without any doubt that, although there are no longer any “pure” bushmen in Kenya today, people resembling bushmen once inhabited the area. But there are hunters and gatherers of other racial groups, too. By way of Kikuyu legends we learn, for example, that the Agumba, a bushman group, originally inhabited the forest regions into which the Kikuyu migrated. Nevertheless, the origins of today’s hunters and gatherers remain unclear. Is what we see today their original culture or have the people returned to this way of life? One thing is certain, however. There has always been a sharp contrast between pastoral nomads and more settled farming peoples in East

Africa. The Kenyan highlands have always been marked by tension between hostile nomads, who belong mainly to stock-raising Hamitic tribes, and the settled Bantu population. On several occasions – right up to the present-day – this contrast has found expression in political conflicts and bloody battles.

Moving on now to consider the artistic achievements of traditional cultures in East Africa, it is remarkable how few examples of fine art we in fact find. This artistic barrenness is often attributed to the influence of the artistically empoverished Hamitic groups who had weakened longstanding traditions of figurative representation. These pastoral peoples, the upper strata of many East African societies, had suppressed all forms of artistic expression in accordance with orthodox Islamic rejection of iconolatry, and because they held manual labour in contempt.

For example, the limited number of masks which have been collected from the majority of East African peoples (the exception being the Makonde of Tanzania) means that one can hardly speak of a traditional art form. In the same way, in the 19th and early 20th centuries, sculpture in most regions was limited to the figurative decoration of staffs, stools, musical instruments and the like. On the other hand it is here (among farmers as well as stockraisers) that we find an abundance of relatively small figures, mostly representations of men. Made using various materials (clay, loam, wood, etc.), these statuettes were used in many different ways. Some had an important role in clearly-defined fertility rites – women would, for example, wear such a doll as an amulet until the first pregnancy. And numerous East African tribes used loam figures as visual aids in bush schools. Using these figures, noninitiated boys and girls would learn about behaviour suitable to community life. As in all of Africa, certain figures of East African origin were credited with magical powers to protect the wearer from evil spirits and disease.

And so, although we find only a modest amount of pictorial arts among the peoples of East Africa, the frequently referred to "artistic barrenness" is, as a few concrete examples clearly show, an exaggeration.

The **Swahili,** an urban culture along the East African coast.

The area in which the Swahili culture originated, and throughout which it spread, extends along some 3,000 km (nearly 2,000 miles) of coastline from Mogadiscio, present-day capital of Somalia, as far as Sofala in Mozambique. The islands off the coast of Kenya (among others, the Bajun islands and the Lamu archipelago) form part of a coral barrier which lessens the swell of the Indian Ocean, thus creating a calm and navigable natural channel along the coast. The name Swahili comes from the Arabic "sahil", meaning coast, and originally meant "coastal inhabitants". The Swahili do not form an ethnic unit, however, since the population of the coastal region comprises Bantu, Arab, Persian, Indian and Indonesian peoples. Their language, Swahili, is a Bantu language which has over the years borrowed a great many Arabic words. Settlements along the East African coast were mentioned as early as in the 2nd century A. D. (in the "Periplus Maris Erythraei", a seafarer's manual) and from the 7th to the 12th centuries, the east coast experienced a boom under Arab influence.

The Lamu archipelago off the coast of northern Kenya has always been a bastion of the arts and crafts. And yet in all the many works published about African art, the arts and crafts of the East African coast are only ever briefly discussed. The fact that these traditional arts and crafts are sinking ever more into oblivion means that a study of this subject will, at some time in the future, unfortunately no longer be possible.

Of the decorative techniques which once flourished here, lacquerware and inlaid work are unfortunately no longer produced. Craftsmen who still command such skills today are usually employed almost entirely in restoration work. Painting occurs mainly in the form of boat decoration; commercially produced paints have now ousted traditional dyes. Turning on a lathe is usually carried out mechanically nowadays; only isolated craftsmen will be found working with a hand-operated lathe.

The furnishing of doors and chests with sheet brass can still be seen in Lamu and Mombasa, but wood carving alone remains widespread along the whole length of the coast. The carved doors to be seen in all major towns in the Lamu archipelago, as well as in other coastal towns, are especially impressive. Household appliances and basic utensils (combs, sabots, etc.) are also decoratively carved. Although rarer, ivory carvings are also found, and the quality of the craftmanship is excellent. The oldest-known carved artefacts are approximately 250 years old. Fabrication techniques and ornamentation have barely changed in these 250 years.

It is interesting to note that the complex culture of the coastal population developed independantly and without affecting the cultural development of the peoples inland. The latter were only of interest to the coastal dwellers as suppliers of slaves and ivory, the mainstays of trade along the coast.

In the southern half of Kenya, not far from the coast, the Giryama erect pillars in honour of influential elders (members of a particular cult, witch doctors, etc.). Placed at the head of the grave or as a commemorative monument at the deceased's former dwelling, these wooden pillars either resemble columns with a sculpted capital, or are like plaques with rich chip-carved ornamentation. (In the latter form they are similar in style to the works of the Giryama's neighbours, the Swahili – the latter were deeply influenced by Islam.) When the restless spirit of a dead relative appears in a dream to a mamber of the family (often even years after his death), the wood-carver is instructed to produce such a "kikango". Offerings of food and drink for the dead member of the family are then brought to this simple monument.

The Tiriki, who inhabit an area northeast of Lake Victoria and are the neighbours of the Luo, weave masks covering the whole head using natural fibres. These masks are part of the initiation garments in which youths may appear in the open if they leave their bush camps for a while. Such a mask is first and foremost a veil, a kind of shield for the initiate, who finds himself in an extraordinarily sensitive psychological state at this transitional period in his life – as he abandons childhood and enters manhood. The woven front of the mask is sometimes covered with animal skin.

While East African masks and carved figures cannot really compete with the standard of sculpture achieved in West Africa, basic utensils produced in the area are often very artistic. Items of pottery, basket-weaving, metal forging and pearl embroidery are all of excellent quality. Indeed, even among those items which lack a great deal of figurative ornamentation (on combs, spoons, bowls, etc.) we find beautiful basic forms.

Traditions of body decoration are also of great importance. Ornate jewellery, the dressing of hair, body-painting and tattooing all have an important place in these traditions.

Artistic skill among the African people facilitates the acquisition of foreign trends and techniques. The recent rapid development of decorative wood carving among the Kamba is a good example of the latter.

In the past the Kamba lived predominately as hunters, their speciality being the expert use of bows and poisoned arrows. The poison they used was potent enough to kill an elephant. Consequently, when trade in ivory began to flourish, the Kamba, using their traditional knowledge, soon made a name for themselves over a very wide area as experts in the field.

More recently, however, the Kamba have developed great skills as carvers. The growth of tourism in East Africa meant an increase in the demand for wood carvings and the Kamba were quick to recognise this opening in the market and began to produce a wide range of curios of varying quality. Wamanyu, almost exactly halfway between Machakos and Kitui, is the centre of this flourishing trade.

Traders from among the Kamba travel extensively in East Africa, in the area of the Rift Valley lakes and as far as Zaire, selling these wares. They are always to be seen in places frequented by tourists – in hotels, airports and on the main streets of tourist centres. In addition, the Kamba are recognised as talented mechanics. During colonial rule large numbers of Kamba were recruited into the police force and into the "King's African Riffles"; they continue to make up an important part of the Kenyan army today. Among the many and varied professions needed in the military, that of the mechanic plays an important role – and it was in this particular field that the Kamba excelled. Military life not only provided for the wanderlust of the Kamba but also offered a welcome improvement in the meagre living they had earned from agriculture up to that time.

Kenya's north, mile after monotonous mile of stones, sand, heat and aridity, is a most desolate area. The bare red earth of the hot plains is littered with volcanic rubble, the horizon marked by the silhouettes of distant mountains. With annual precipitation of less than 300 mm (less than 12 ins), only sparse vegetation grows in this area, and trees are found only in wadies and oases, and in moister elevated areas. At the centre of this bleak dry area lies **Lake Turkana,** stretching 250 km southwards from Kenya's northern border. The beautiful, crystal-clear waters of the lake (Lake Rudolf until 1976) were discovered by Teleki and Höhnel in 1899. Like the other lakes in the Rift Valley, Lake Turkana is subject to significant dehydration.

As already mentioned, man made Kenya's north his own very early in history; numerous finds of the remains of hominids were made in the immediate vicinity of Lake Turkana. In spite of this, very little is known about the aboriginal population of the lake or about their culture. Centuries ago, tall, slim, dark-skinned Nilo-Hamitic peoples migrated into these arid regions from the north and settled in them. In the course of time these peoples adapted to ecological conditions in their own particular environment and so came to differ from each other both psychologically and culturally.

Aturkwen, the land of the Turkana people also lies on this bleak plain. The majority of the **Turkana** live as **nomadic pastoralists** today, although as recently as 200 years ago they were involved in crop cultivation in eastern Uganda. They probably migrated to northwest Kenya some 150 years ago, in time becoming one of the most important nomadic tribes there.

The freedom of movement of each individual member of the Turkana is subject to no restrictions, be these in the form of either political or territorial divisions. Clans are of no particular significance but the Turkana do have a defined class system based on age. (It is interesting to note here that circumcision, common among most pastoralist groups, is not part of their initiation ceremonies.) In addition to age sets, all the men are divided into two groups, the "Stones" and the "Leopards". If the father is a member of the "Stones" his son automatically joins the "Leopards", and vice versa. Each of these groups has its own particular style of dress and ornamentation, its own initiation ceremonies, and its own social hierarchy.

Like other East African nomads, the Turkana knew no chieftains. Only in times of war and for their raids which took place fairly regularly would a leader be chosen. Even today, the power of the District Chiefs (these are appointed by the Kenyan government) is based less upon their political office than upon their personal wealth. The District Commissioner in Lodwar is the highest administrative authority in Turkana-land today. But the basic lack of interest in politics and administration among the Turkana people has undergone no significant change since Kenyan independence.

A Turkana man's greatest interest is still his livestock: camels, sheep, goats and donkeys. Milk, meat and blood obtained from these animals provide essential nourishment, but the importance of Turkana animals goes far beyond such basic needs. As the source of moral values and emotions, animals accompany the Turkana man through each phase of his life. Through his animals he is nearer to his god, Akuj; with animals he grieves and celebrates; payment and atonement are made with livestock; a man's animals are the very foundation of his existence. A man's position and prestige depend on the number of animals he possesses. As is the case with most East African nomads, quantity is more important than quality. The killing of large animals constitutes a religious and social occasion, and so for daily food requirements only goats, sheep and donkeys are slaughtered. All cultural achievements are linked in some way with the rearing of livestock. Work and hardship do not play a large part in the lives of Turkana men. In fact the warrior class, the "moran" have been more or less "unemployed" since the Pax Britannica. They spend most of their time today taking part in sporting competitions and celebrations, and carrying out raids on other pastoral groups in order to steal cattle (often a man has to pay up to 50 animals as bride price and so has to resort to such raids – he sees his act not as theft but as the taking back of what is rightly his, his ancestors having been given all the cattle in the world). A great deal of time is also devoted to dress and ornamentation. Very characteristic of the latter is the elaborate way in which the hair of young Turkana men is dressed. Thin stands of hair are plaited and the braids interwoven. Subsequently the hair is smeered with red or blue-grey coloured paste. Once dry, such a coiffure lasts for several weeks, since hand-carved neck stools support the head, and therefore protect the hair, during sleep.

A Turkana woman enjoys a great deal of respect and attention since the welfare of the family depends upon her work. She organizes and prepares food, builds huts, makes clothes and articles of ornamentation, often spends hours carrying heavy loads of water from the nearest water hole, and is responsible for the upbringing of children and the rearing of small animals. Turkana women wear beaded aprons made of goatskin which reach down to the ankles at the back. A linen wrap is often worn over this apron. Strings of beads have now replaced the traditional decoration which consisted of finely-worked disk beads made of ostrich shell, fruits and antelope bones. Jewellery worn around the neck is still indicative of the esteem in which a woman is held and the wealth of her husband.

Formerly the men wore no form of clothing; nowadays they wrap a piece of cloth around themselves, knotting this with great flair at the right shoulder.

As a result of repeated droughts in the last few years, many families have lost their herds and have settled on the western shores of Lake Turkana. Here they live from fishing, a way of life which they once scorned but which has been encouraged and sponsored by the Kenyan government.

This is not to say that fishing on Lake Turkana is a recent innovation. It has long been practised on the volcanic islands and south shore by the **Elmolo.** The Elmolo, the "smallest tribe of Africa", are often thought to be the descendants of the prehistoric fishing people who were once widespread in the area. The present-day culture of the Elmolo is marked by a complete adaptation to the ways of their neighbours, the Samburu. For example, animals have now replaced the two rafts made from palm trunks which were traditionally paid for a bride.

The animals of the lake are as important to the Elmolo as livestock are to the nomads, representing far more than just a source of food. A goatskin and wood amulet representing a fish will, for example, guarantee a good catch. The hippopotamus hunt is a most important occasion, especially now that these animals have grown so rare. The women honour successful hunters by adorning them with their own necklaces.

The cultures of the Turkana and the Elmolo have proved themselves to be relatively stable. Living as they do, well away from the "civilized" centres of East Africa, their traditional way of life still functions and the long-standing structures of their society have remained intact. In fact, the ecological structure of each group rules out any fundamental changes.

The culture of the **Galla,** a people who migrated from Ethiopia to north central Kenya, has a great deal in common with that of other African peoples for whom the raising of livestock is an essential element. It was in the 16th and 17 centuries, when their military power was at its greatest, that the Galla moved from the highlands and began to spread over a much larger area. It now seems that this large-scale migration came to an end only when the mouth of the Tana river in the south and the Sudan in the west had been reached. The "pure" Galla call themselves **Borana** in order to differentiate between themselves and the people who already inhabited the country into which they moved. It is no longer possible to accurately reconstruct just how the spread of the Galla, and therefore the formation of the individual tribes, took place.

Like the Turkana, the Galla are always thought of as cattle-herding **pastoralists**. In the highlands of Ethiopia they did, however, cultivate barley. This is why barley is thought of both in the highlands (where it usually grows) and in lower-lying areas as the most sacred fruit of the earth. Created together with cattle, it was meant to be used for sacrificial offerings. In the same way, highland cattle and long-tailed highland sheep are not only economically important but also have a significant role in the religion of the Galla. Only cows and sheep are used in sacrificial rites; beside them, animals common in more low-lying areas (camels, goats) are of no significance.

It is interesting to note that although the Borana have been in the lowlands for the past 200 years they still have not come around to breeding camels. Instead, they continue to buy them from the Somali for use as pack animals.

The Borana believe that they were the first born of all Galla, but it must be pointed out that they know very little about any other groups. And of all the Galla, it is the Borana who have retained very little historical consciousness. Even up to a hundred years ago they were still migrating through the unending savanna westwards as far as Lake Turkana and southwards to the edge of Masai land. They speak a Cushitic language and are representatives of an Eastern Hamitic culture.

Former vassal tribes like the Gabra in northern Kenya are now entirely liberated. As early as during colonial rule the Gabra were awarded pasture lands in northern Kenya stretching as far east as Lake Turkana and to Marsabit in the south. It was in this way that the Borana were separated from their brother Galla farther north. Three enclaves, Liban, Marsabit and Garba Tulla, are all that remain there of this once so widespread people.

In the savannas of Kenya the culture of the Borana moved further and further away from that of other Galla peoples, having come under the influence of the Borana's new neighbours – above all, the Somali and the Masai. The most important change was the total abandonment of tillage. Like the Masai, the Borana lived solely from their livestock, the latter finding ample grazing in the endless savannas of the region, and the aridity of the Borana steppe having precluded the settlement of farmers almost entirely. In more fertile regions such settlement had of course meant a reduction in the land available to herdsmen. The breeding of livestock (which has an important place in the lives of the Borana in any case) ousted tillage to such an extent that, even when they came face to face with crop farmers on their own lands, they were not able to decide in favour of its readoption, deeming it beneath their dignity to plant or sow. Since Borana land belonged to everyone, a man could choose to settle in any place where he found ample pasture lands and water holes. Today's extensive settlements and organized crop farming make such a way of life impossible.

Of all the Galla peoples, the Borana have the richest culture in a material sense. This is as true of the variety of expression which their culture finds as of their own close link with the intellectual and social facets of this culture. Indeed among no other Galla peoples do the different forms of expression used by each cultural activity form such a complete and unified whole.

The gada system was the central institution in the life of the Galla. Over forty years of life each expression made by the individual was dependent upon his belonging to this all-encompassing social order. The gada system was the sum of all laws ruling the life of the Galla. Despite a general tendancy towards the disintegration of the gada system, traces of it are still to be found among peoples who have a Cushitic language.

While other Galla peoples choose to live in single huts, the Borana prefer hamlets comprising around twenty farmsteads for their human and cattle populations. The animals are housed in kraals and the Borana live in adjacent huts. These hamlets are surrounded by a protective thorn fence. The villagers form an economic community which changes, however, when the hamlets are moved to other pastures – this used to happen about twice a year.

The construction of the kraal with its tall, upright thorn tree branches is the only task carried out by the men. (The most sacred part of this animal enclosure is the outer door where the head of the family stands in the mornings or evenings and greets the incoming or outgoing livestock with whispered words of blessing.)

Other work on the construction of the house is carried out by the women. A man owns as many houses as he has wives. The low, irregular shape of a Borana house means that it is often hard to tell it from a haystack. The orderly interior with its fine finishing touches, furniture and utensils stands in sharp contrast to the simple exterior of the hut.

Containers for milk and butter, and milking utensils are given special attention. Most important of all is the milking pot. The Borana ideally make these vessels from giraffe skin since this is harder-wearing than cowhide. Vessels of woven grass later became as characteristic of the Galla as these leather bowls. The manufacture of woven grass bowls is very complicated, the grass being woven so closely that it is watertight. Cowrie shells are sewn onto the lids of these ornamental vessels and they are hung on the walls using decorative bands. Under Somali influence the Borana have become masters of the craft of carving wooden vessels in a remarkably rich variety of forms. However, the leather sack is still the most widely-used receptacle for all kinds of utensils.

Goatskin used to be the most popular material for women's clothing. The government campaigned successfully to replace skins with cloth, and to do away with the very elaborate pearl and metal jewellery of the women.

Traditionally the Borana never wash and the only time that water touches their skin is when it rains. All Galla considered washing to be not only unnecessary but also dangerous – they believed that the skin was "weakened" through contact with water and, more seriously, that animals, unable to recognise the smell of their masters, would become shy and perhaps even aggressive. Their attitude to cleanliness as Westerners know it could easily be misconstrued as a lack of attention to personal hygiene and grooming, but this would be to disregard the great deal of time which is devoted to appearance. It is a matter of course, for example, to use as many cosmetic preparations as possible. Such preparations include the application of rancid butter to the skin and the smoking of garments with different sorts of wood and resin. The use of butter makes for silky-smooth, shining skin, which is in turn highlighted by the Galla's incredibly white teeth. Men as well as women rub their teeth constantly with a stripped piece of a particular kind of hard wood.

The Borana have long since lost their warlike spirit and are now amongst the most passive and pacifist of ethnic groups. Their decline began in the middle of the 19th century as the Somali, moving ever-farther westwards, engaged them in regular skirmishes and then defeated them decisively in 1870.

The concept of ownership or demarcation of tribal land means nothing to either the Borana or the Somali, something which has led to a great deal of conflict between these people.

The **Somali** of northeast Kenya are a people who are never at rest. This, together with their apparent fertility, has meant that these people have spread over a larger and larger area in the course of the centuries. This expansion has never been checked – not even nowadays with the establishment of defined ethnic territories. Every year the Somali move farther west in search of fresh pastures encroaching upon Rendile, Samburu and Borana land.

Nomadic tribal groups of Somali usually comprise five or six families linked by blood relationship or marriage. These groups usually move on at intervals of two months, i. e. when pastures are bare and wells dry.

For the Somali, nomadism isn't just a way of life but a form of culture, too. The Somali were converted to Islam by travelling scholars as early as in the 9th century but they have retained a great many of their native beliefs. They venerate everything which lives – animals, plants, woods, rivers, lightning, the wind. They believe the snake to be the father of the world. Water, land and livestock are seen as their god's gifts to nomads. It is not man but nature which stands at the centre of their world view.

The **Tana Galana** people of today, wholly Islamic in faith, and culturally almost identical to the Somali, are a mere shadow of the powerful race they once were but which had begun to disappear even before 1870 in the wake of the more powerful Somali and Masai.

Few ethnic groups in all of Africa are as well-known as the **Masai** of Kenya and Tanzania. Their unusual appearance and elegant posture have made them *the* African people – they feature on the front cover of travel brochures and have come to represent all that is exotic and different in Africa.

Pastoral life has always had a romantic charm for town and city dwellers and the Masai live up to visions of the warrior herdsman leaning on his spear and looking out over mile after mile of steppe. And yet the Masai are in fact far from typical of the culture of the East African cattle-breeder. This leads to many misconceptions. The first of these is the belief that pastoralists are wholly dependent on their herds, the second that they raise just one kind of animal.

In reality, most are also involved in some kind of arable farming, or at least have dependents who carry out this work for them. Secondly they will usually have a not inconsiderable number of other animals (sheep and goats and larger animals such as donkeys and camels) as well as their cattle.

The Masai and Turkana are different in that they do not practise any kind of arable farming. They do, however, keep sheep as well as beef. Here we come face to face with another misconception, i. e. that pastoralists are independent and self-sufficient. This is far from the truth. In western Uganda and northern Tanzania the cattle-owning aristocracy make use of a class of conquered Bantu farmers. In any case the pastoralists are very much dependent on farming neighbours and tradesmen not only for basic foodstuffs but also for those items of value which are a necessary part of their economy and their culture.

Although less apparently dependent on their neighbours, the Masai also have their own serving class. It is the Dorobo or Asi who are responsible for the slaughtering of animals and the circumcision of young warriors. In the same way, a group of smiths take care of weapon and jewellery manufacture. The Masai are becoming ever more dependent on traders from whom they buy wire and metal as well as certain skins, furs, feathers and horns (all are an indispensable part of their clothing and equipment).

Another misconception is that environmental conditions were decisive in the development of a nomadic, cattle-herding way of life. In fact, the region inhabited by the Masai was also suitable for agriculture and hunting and gathering. From this we can deduce that the breeding of cattle, although the focal point of their existence, was not their only occupation. (The Masai also hunt and gather – they use animal skins as ornamentation and as exchange goods with which to acquire other essentials, and they are particularly fond of wild honey.)

The final misconception to be destroyed is that all pastoralists are always nomads. Although the keeping of cattle presupposes a certain mobility, the freedom of movement of the herdsman is in fact much less than is often supposed. Most never move from a particular area nowadays, and when lack of water and pasture make a move absolutely necessary, they simply establish a number of temporary camps for livestock and those herding the cattle.

Many aspects of Masai culture are to be found among other pastoralist groups in Africa. So marked was this influence among the Dschagga and Kikuyu that they were referred to as "Masai apes" in early literature.

Today, almost every ethnic group in Africa has adapted in some way to Western styles of dress, and has abandoned traditional weapons. Often it is unfortunately only when tourists are around and there is a chance of some supplementary income from photographers that one sees the traditional and beautiful leather clothing and is reminded of the nobility and timelessness of Africa and her people.

Reflections on **African music** usually proceed from two basic assumptions. The first of these is that music is a means of communication much like the spoken word. Although music can never be as clear and understandable as language, it remains a vital form of cultural expression, one which calls forth certain reactions from the listener. The second assumption is that there exists a multiplicity of possible ways of interpreting music. The fundamental tenets of a group of people form the basis of a particular interpretation.

The basis of the predominate sound of East Africa is not very complex but does encompass the sounds of set musical devises (conventional percussion and stringed instruments, etc.) as well as those of undefined devises (improvised use of troughs, etc. as percussion instruments). For a lack of musical instruments has never prevented general music-making among the African people, and this music can be seen as a product of a particular environment and way of life. Axeblades and other tools, oars, sticks, dry seeds inside hollow containers, all are employed in order to find a suitable working rhythm, for example, music shared by people working together helping to lighten the load of a particular task.

We have already seen that there is immense diversity among the peoples of East Africa – whether from the point of view of culture, religious beliefs, language, day-to-day life, and even colour of skin. Generalizations only serve to confuse therefore and, in the face of so many different nationalities and ethnic groups (each with its own language) in any one area, problems of communication between people become only too clear. For the very same reason, it is difficult to single out, and arrive at an understanding of, individual musical traditions.

Language plays an important part in East African music, since even a perfectly rendered song will not have the desired effect if the language of the song is unknown to the listener. For, although the entertainment value of such a piece of music cannot be overlooked, the meaning of the sung word remains decisive and, in order to understand the music, we must understand the language.

Instrumental music (featuring flutes, xylophones, trumpets) rarely includes vocal accompaniment. However, if the name of the piece of music is known and the listener is familiar with the language of the region in which a particular instrument originated, then he/she will be able to pick out the words "spoken" by that instrument. This kind of music is fairly common in West Africa but is rare in East Africa except perhaps among the Ganda and Soga of Uganda, who do in fact often play flutes, xylophones, panpipes and trumpets.

African xylophones and lamellophones tell us a great deal about the African tone system. One of the most original of African instruments, the lamellophone consists of metal tongues of varying length which span a bridge and are secured to the top of a hollowed-out wooden box-resonator.

Sound formation and timbre are important aspects of music all over Africa. A "pure" tone, completely free of vibrato, while being an ideal of Western music, has no place in the aesthetic ideals of African musicians and singers. For them a tone should not be pure but should have a character all of its own. For this reason it is almost impossible to do justice to the nuances and chromatic variations achieved by African singers in any notation of their music according to Western systems.

Western audiences associate all African music first and foremost with rhythm. It's safe to say that an interest in African music is usually kindled by a fascination with its complex rhythms. Yet there are kinds of East African music in which we find only traces of stereotypical African rhythms. Drums, for example, do not feature in the music of regions where no larger trees are found. In addition, the wealth of melodic music in Africa cannot be ignored if we are to arrive at a true picture of traditional African music. It is above all among peoples who sing without any kind of drum accompaniment that we find highly-developed melodies which are far more complex than those among groups for whom the inclusion of a drum is the usual practice. The Somali, Turkana and Masai in Kenya and the Hime in Uganda play intricate, flowing melodies and sing these lentamente.

Luo-speaking peoples, on the other hand, have melodies where rhythm is once again the essential element. The music of Bantu peoples (the Ganda and Soga are good examples) includes melodies which are both flowing and rhythmical but which from an instrumental point of view are definitely allegro. But all the many different kinds of melodies have one common factor – they are generally short and are repeated regularly, making them easy to learn, even for non-Africans.

Careful analysis reveals that traditional African melodies are based on defined tonal systems. On the whole, we can also say that outside influences have had little effect on the tone systems and playing techniques in East Africa. Instrumentalists must be given credit for having remained faithful to traditional music, especially as this has unfortunately not been the case with vocal music. On the East African coast, melodies show a distinct Arab influence; inland, Western influences are evident.

Often one comes across African schoolchildren singing traditional African songs using the Western diatonic scale. In doing so they usually replace the major second or minor third of the original with a minor second in order not to sing in the same way as uneducated people or simple villagers. This attitude represents a danger to African music since often even the teacher is no longer able to differentiate between the African and the foreign scales if both are sung in an African language.

Outside influences are especially obtrusive in the field of melody. In other areas (e. g. that of rhythm) new trends come up against greater resistance – resistance which is almost impossible to break down quite simply because of the superiority of African rhythm.

Rhythm is the basis of music all over Africa. In East Africa some groups prefer quick, fervent rhythms while others opt for slow, elegant rhythms which are so rich in themselves that they do not require any kind of vocal or instrumental accompaniment. For the purposes of dance, the drum is the most important instrument in East Africa as well as elsewhere, although in comparison with West Africa, relatively few drums are used at any one time.

In earlier times a particular rhythm beaten on drums would have been be used to transmit news over long distances, to call people to work, to warn of danger, to announce ceremonies, and to give members of a particular clan notice of a marriage or any other important occurence. Nowadays, however, rhythm is no longer used as a means of communication.

Many have expressed concern lest social changes in Africa mean the demise of native African music. But the fact that African music has survived so many changes in the course of history and has always shown so much creative vitality and ability to adapt to changes gives grounds for hope that it will continue to live on well beyond the twentieth century.

# The Kenyan Economy

Tourism is becoming an ever more important branch of the Kenyan economy, since it brings a great deal of foreign currency into the country. It is for this reason that Kenya has built up a **tourist infrastructure** which is highly-developed, especially when compared with that of similarly developed countries in Africa.

Since Kenya has almost no natural resources, the economy is based primarily upon **agriculture.** Yet only 18% of the total land area of Kenya is suitable for agriculture, and irrigation is essential. The narrow coastal strip, which enjoys a moist climate, is fertile; the steppe behind this coastal strip can be used for a certain amount of cattle grazing; the highlands around Nairobi are again fertile; but between the coast and highlands there is a huge area of savanna and dry bush which is only very sparcely populated. It is in this area that the animals of Africa live, constituting as they do a most precious gift of nature but one which must be protected from Man if it is to survive.

Kenya as an agricultural country lives from its exports of coffee and tea, sisal, fruits, wheat, cotton and wool, and beef. Most of these are products which were already exported by Europeans during the period when they had control of the Kenyan economy and wished to maintain it. After independence, the black government was confronted here too with problems which were far from easy to solve. It had, and still has, to tread carefully and cautiously if it is to do away with discrepancies in educational and living standards among blacks and whites, and bridge the gap between rich and poor without destroying the traditional cultures of the Kenyan people.

It remains a point of fact that a great many Kenyans still have to learn to use those "instruments" of industry and administration which were employed by white colonialists and immigrants to shape their land. It is only by doing so that the Kenyan people will be able to gain most from the already well-established social and economic structures. This is a thorny problem but one which Kenya shows every sign of mastering.

There is a fixed programme of foreign **development aid** in Kenya. It provides agricultural and industrial advisors, vets and economics experts, water experts and nurses, computer specialists and teachers for apprentices. They have been joined in the last few years by tourism advisors and experts in the hotel business.

For many Kenyans the statement that Kenya is one of the few African countries which is enjoying a kind of **economic miracle** is reality. These are the people who are better off now than before political independence, who have for example obtained their own plot of land which they used to cultivate for one of the big

## Tourism

In Kenya, tourism now brings just as much foreign currency into the country as is earned by coffee exports. But this fact does not mean that the country is resting on its laurels. Tourism – as is well-known – is a tender plant in need of continuous care, much like the coffee tree, "Coffea arabica". For this reason development aid from abroad also encompasses calling on tourism experts to help with the development of the tourism industry in Kenya.

The biggest attraction for most tourists is not so much the marvellous beaches as the wild animals in the national parks. Today, about 80,000 Kenyans live directly or indirectly from tourism. The Kenyan Ministry of Tourism estimates that 500,000 people visited Kenya in 1985, many being repeat visitors. Of those booking with a tour operator, well over half made at least one safari trip into the game reserves.

On the coast (and particularly south of Mombasa) there are more than 30 hotels, with accommodation for about 4,000, on mile after mile of sandy beaches which are almost as white as flour. These hotels are not only well-appointed; they are also an ideal starting-point for safaris, particularly into both parts of Tsavo National Park and Amboseli Park.

(white) landowners. However, the economic miracle has been achieved at the cost of a new kind of dependence – economic dependence. On a stroll through the streets of Nairobi – a city with a distinctly European atmosphere – it is not very difficult to see that many of the products on offer come from abroad. And many companies with registered offices in Kenya send their profits back home. Only the wages stay in Kenya, and then only when Kenyans are employed. In return, Kenyans have to pay a high price for popular foreign products, and have to pay with money their country earns with its exports. However, whereas foreign industrial and consumer goods get more and more expensive, coffee prices on the world market are falling. The cash Kenya receives for its coffee exports is not enough to pay for essential imports. One of the most essential is oil: in 1980, Kenya had to use its total income from coffee exports to buy oil. Urgent projects – aimed at building schools. roads, and living accommodation, installing water mains, digging wells, etc. – had to take a back seat.

However, Kenya seems to be on the way to improvement: as much as 15% of industrial and consumer goods are now made in Kenya – much more than in most other African countries. In spite of many difficulties, Kenya has become something of an industrial centre in East Africa. The foundation stone for this was actually laid during the colonial period, when Kenya, together with Uganda and Tanzania, had a com-

# Coffee

"Arabica" coffee is held in high esteem throughout the world because of its excellent quality. It is expensive because it demands certain kinds of soil and climate, and because it has to be handled particularly carefully. It is an ideal crop for farmers with only a small piece of land who can devote a great deal of time and attention to its cultivation. More than a quarter of a million farmers plant coffee-shrubs, and there are also about 1,000 plantations which, however, only provide about a third of Kenya's total coffee crop. All in all, the total area planted with coffee-shrubs is only about 1,000 sq. km (roughly 400 sq. miles). More than one million Kenyans make a living out of coffee: if world market prices drop, their existence is in danger, the whole Kenyan economy being subject to the same variations. After all, Kenya's coffee exports account for a third of all Kenya's exports. On the whole, however, it is very difficult to sample the real taste of Kenyan coffee. Because it is so precious, it is used for blends and to improve the taste of other, cheaper, types of coffee of which there is no shortage. Whoever wishes to enjoy genuine Kenyan coffee will almost have to travel to Kenya...

mon market it controlled. Nairobi and Mombasa (the latter the most important port in the region) developed into business and industrial centres. In 1977, when the common market broke apart, Kenya had to look around for new markets.

Increased assistance had to be given to important branches of industry because there was no cooperation from the neighbouring countries of Uganda and Tanzania. For instance, an important oil refinery was built in Mombasa to cover Kenya's own requirements; and the Bamburi cement works is doing good business with the Middle East and other African countries. The "Made in Kenya" sign is indicative of a high standard of goods: textiles and tyres are manufactured here, cross-country vehicles and lorries are built in Kenyan factories, construction steel is produced from scrap, and paper is made from West Kenyan trees and some of it is even exported. Foodstuffs and numerous articles of everyday use are also manufactured (usually in fairly small factories) – welcome competition to the more expensive foreign products.

Factories of course need energy to work, and 85% of Kenya's energy is obtained from oil. This closes the vicious circle: too expensive oil pushes the price of domestically-manufactured products up, and the balance of trade suffers. Small wonder then that construction work on dams is given top priority in Africa. A good example of this is the Tana river project in Kenya. By building dams and therefore establishing reliable sources of domestic **hydroelectricity,** Kenya's dependence on expensive foreign oil will be lessened.

Agriculture and cattle-breeding can only thrive in those areas where conditions for them are naturally suitable, or where they have been improved over the years by farmers. This is the case, for example, northwest of Nairobi, in the direction of the equator, where you would normally only expect scorching sun or jungle: beyond Naivasha, luscious pastures can be seen with well-fed European dairy cattle grazing on them, and beyond Nakuru, where the mountains reach a height of 9,600 ft (3,200 m), we have the same picture of an almost European pastoral landscape. On reaching the equator, we stand in the midst of wheatfields, the golden-yellow wheat waving in the breeze. And a further surprise: the air is cool and of course rarified at this height.

Near Kericho (west of Nakuru in the direction of Lake Victoria) whole plantations of deep green tea shrubs appear. And under Mt. Kenya, which watches, snow-capped, over them, there are the extensive coffee plantations with Kenya's most precious export article.

But with the exception of these fertile highlands and the moist coastal region, the country is bare and dry, two thirds of the total area being semi-desert. The Nairobi – Mt. Kenya – Mt. Elgon triangle attracted the first Britons as early as the beginning of this century, because it was the centre of the fertile zone and had (and still has) a

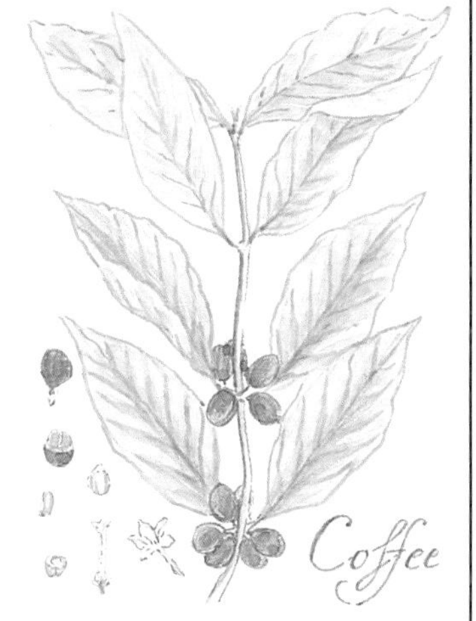


pleasant climate. They founded their first British colony here, which is why the area soon came to be known as the "white highlands". A white thorn in black African flesh.

Things remained this way until independence, when most farming land and property had to be handed over to Kenyans. Not all of it, however: some large farms and plantations still belong to whites. But in the normal course of events, the European owners had to agree to hand over the land they had appropriated to the Kenyan government (compensation was paid to them for this land). The government then gave this land either to big cooperatives made up of several small farmers, or to individual African owners. This was a resettlement programme which was so costly that it could

# Foreign Aid to Kenya

Kenya's political and economic record since independence has been a good one – far better, in fact, than many other African nations which seemed to have more favourable prospects (in view of their natural resources, etc.). Kenya is an agricultural land, 70% of exports stemming from agriculture. In 1980 Kenya was, after Brazil and Tanzania, the third-largest producer of sisal (48,000 tonnes). Between 1970 and 1980 coffee production was increased by almost 100%, tea production by over 100%. A well-developed tourist industry also contributes substantially to the economy. But political stability and apparent properity (especially in the capital) do not mean that we are talking about a prosperous land. Per capita income for 1980 was estimated at US$ 420 (in 1984 the per capita income threshold, indicating eligibility for grant aid, was raised from US$ 405 to US$ 795).

The United States is currently the largest bilateral donar to Kenya. Development assistance in the financial year 1984 from loans and grants was an estimated $ 90 million, with an additional $ 20 million in the form of food aid (Food for Peace). The main aim is to promote broad-based economic development, the three main objectives being the reduction of population growth, the increase of rural production, employment and income, and the improvement of basic social services. Most work is therefore done among small farmers and the rural landless, and is concentrated on the high-potential agricultural land in west Kenya and in the arid regions such as Kitui District in the Eastern Province. In addition, the Peace Corps provides volunteer workers in the fields of agriculture and education, and the U.S. Information Service maintains a library and educational office in Nairobi and conducts cultural exchanges.

British Overseas Aid to Kenya in 1984 amounted to £ 38 million. Aid takes the form of assistance in establishing new, or expanding existing, production and infrastructure facilities – for example, contributing to the construction of a hydroelectric plant at Kiambere on the Tana river. Financial aid is also given to ease balance of payments deficits exacerbated by the need to import food after drought. Technical co-operation provides manpower, training, and consultancy services; scholarships exist whereby Kenyans can train either in Britain or overseas. In 1984 Britain had an important role in the development of sector aid in Kenya. The sectoral approach means that emphasis is laid on one particular area (in Kenya's case, agriculture and railways) and that the government is encouraged to make considerable long-term economic adjustments in this area.

(Figures from: U.S. Dept. of State, Background Notes on the Countries of the World, 1985 Foreign and Commonwealth Office of the U.K., Britain's Overseas Aid in 1984) only be implemented with the help of the Britons themselves, and other nations which had been closely involved in Africa.

It was of course feared that these expropriations would have predominantly negative consequences. However, this was not, or hardly, the case, a fact which was doubtlessly attributable in no small way to Kenya's policy of political neutrality – a policy which enables Kenya to be characterized as politically stable. Although the total area given over to agriculture decreased in size, overall production grew considerably, particularly as a result of intensive utilization by small farmers.

Even such programmes have hardly been able to bring about any change in the central problem affecting the millions of small farmers that Kenya has. In the central and western highlands, where farmers have settled in large numbers, their families (usually quite large) have to live off less than one hectare (2.5 acres) of land. Their proficiency and tenacity are almost unsurpassed in Africa – they really do extract everything the soil has to give – but they can be happy if they can feed their families; there is hardly anything left over to sell. The chief crops are maize and bananas, beans and sweet potatoes, and other vegetables which thrive under intensive farming methods. Crops grown specifically for export or sale are coffee and tea, and a cultivated chrysanthemum, pyrethrum, from which an important insecticide is produced which harms neither man nor cattle.

Fertile land can no longer be increased, but the population – and, concomitantly, the number of farmers without their own piece of land – is growing continuously. This is Kenya's central problem, one which it will have to deal with in the near future (work has in fact already begun). Industrialization can only be a solution when the energy problem has been solved, which in turn means ending Kenya's dependence on oil. Otherwise, Kenya will just be caught in a never-ending vicious circle.

# Food and Drink

A pleasant reminder of the fact that the British were Kenya's first colonial settlers is given at **breakfast**: "Early Morning Tea" will await you, together with a substantial breakfast (frequently from a buffet) including bacon and eggs, porridge and cornflakes, toast and marmelade, and enriched by a wide variety of tropical fruits and fruit juices. **Lunch** is a fairly modest affair, available hot or cold, and frequently in hotels from a buffet for a fixed price; even in fairly simple restaurants there are at least three courses. Barring earthquakes, the next meal is afternoon tea, with biscuits or tiny sandwiches to go with exquisite teas. **"Dinner"** is usually a festive occasion.

At all events, Kenyan cuisine, a result of African, Persian, Indian, Chinese, Japanese, Italian and

French influences, is never boring. The selection of dishes available, except in the lodges, is extremely varied. Although the **lodges** do offer specialities such as zebra cutlets or gazelle chops, the selection is otherwise modest – for purely practical reasons such as transport and storage.

The quality and quantity of the food on offer are, by the way, higher than the price would lead you to expect.

Perch ("tilapia") comes from Lake Victoria, trout from mountain streams, and fish dishes in numerous variations are available on the coast. Unsurpassed in taste is Molo mutton, which seldom comes from Molo. "Kitumbua" is a tasty kind of cake from roasted rice; "papadom" and "chipatee", two Indian bread specialities, are a more familiar sight, however. Cafés offer "samosas" – meat-filled pasties baked in oil. Asian cafés in the side streets of Mombasa sell unbelievably hot and unusual delicacies such as "Bombay chowder" and "chana bateta", both of Indian origin, as is apparent from the names. The "fire" they burn inside you is extinguished on the spot with the juice of the passion fruit.

And what do the Kenyans themselves like to eat? There is an endless supply of tropical fruit. **Bananas,** originally from Southeast Asia but now grown in Kenya, are very popular and a staple food of the people. Whether yellow or red, the smaller they are, the tastier (or sweeter). Green bananas are cooked, mashed and made into "matoke". Apart from bananas, the main food source is sweet **maize**, from which "posho" is made. This dish is complemented by fruit or meat gravy. Millet and beans, sorghum, yam and cassava roots are further ingredients of African dishes such as "irio" and "ugali". You ought to try them at least once!

**Wine** drinkers will have to make do with European brands, which are anything but cheap; African "wines" are usually made from fruit, roots, etc. What does taste delicious and is thirst-quenching at the same time is coconut milk ("madafu"), either on its own or mixed with rum, but at all events drunk from a coconut shell and through a straw, of course. Palm wine ("mnazi" or "tembo"), which is really a spirit, has a curious taste.

The English left behind them a good tradition of quality **tea** production. East African coffee is a delicacy, although it is not always prepared in the way Westerners are used to drinking it... but then you are in Africa!

In the towns, **tap water** can usually be drunk without second thoughts. If this is not the case, you will find a flask of distilled or mineral water in your hotel room. For cleaning teeth, tapwater can be used everywhere without hesitation.

Kenyan beer brewed from bananas ("pombe") or millet ("malwa") is probably not what Westerners are used to. However, Kenyan beer brewed in the European way is now available in several versions, is cheap and palatable, and just the right thing for quenching safari thirst. Imported beer is more expensive and not necessarily better.

# Kenya from A to Z

The following list includes some places of interest which are just across the border in Tanzania.

**Aberdare National Park** (E4): This is one of the world's highest parks. It is open all year round. As the only road through the park (Nyeri – Naivasha) winds, steep and narrow, as high as 3,000 m (9,850 ft). above sea level, only experienced drivers should attempt this hazardous trip, and then, preferably, in convoy.

**Aberdare Mountain Range** (E4): The highest peaks are Sattimma (3,999 m/13,119 ft) and Kinangop (3,906 m/12,815 ft).

**Amboseli Lake** (E5): For a good part of the year this lake is a dry soda expanse attracting numerous animals and a rich variety of birds. The water level of the lake, which is fed by the melting snows of Mt. Kilimanjaro, has risen as the result of a decrease in the number of acacia trees in the region.

**Amboseli National Park** (E5): See Masai Amboseli Game Reserve.

**Arawale Game Reserve** (G4): A beautiful region which can be visited from Lamu or Malindi in combination with an excursion to the Tana River Primate Reserve.

**The Ark** (E4): Among Kenya cognoscenti, this tree hotel is regarded as the "successor" to the famous "Treetops".

**Arusha National Park** (E5): This park across the border in Tanzania can now be visited again from Kenya. It has a total area of 211 sq. km (81.5 sq. miles) and encompasses the Ngurdoto Crater with its cloud forest, the Momella Lakes, and the montane forest on Mt. Meru. Animals which can be seen here include: elephants, buffalos, Masai giraffes, bushbucks, hippos, rhinos and giant forest hogs.

**Athi River** (E4): This river, south of Nairobi, has formed a deep valley in which the town of the same name is located. Athi is of little interest to the average tourist, but of vital importance to Kenya on account of the cement works there. An important road junction: the A 104 from Nakuru via Nairobi to Arusha in Tanzania (border crossing at Namanga) intersects the A 109 from Nairobi via Vio to Mombasa.

**Bamburi Beach** (F6): This holiday resort on the coast north of Mombasa has a number of good hotels and well-equipped cottages. The Severin Sea Lodge, for example, is famous and very elegant. Kenya's most important cement works, also called Bamburi, is near here.

**Batian Peak** (E4): The highest of Mt. Kenya's three peaks, at 5,199 m (17,057 ft), should only be tackled by climbers with the appropriate alpine experience.

**Blue Lagoon** (G5): The asphalt road from Watamu to Watamu Beach ends just above this crystal-clear lagoon surrounded by coral reefs. There are several hotels and clubs here and virtually every water sport can be enjoyed. Watamu Village, 3 km (2 miles) away, is actually only a handful of huts.

**Boni Reserve** (G4): This reserve bordering on the Dodori Game Reserve northeast of Lamu was created to protect the elephants living in the area.

**Casuarina Point** (G5): This is the administrative centre of delightful Malindi Marine Park – well worth a visit! The coral gardens here are reputed to be the loveliest on the coast, and they are also among the most accessible. You can charter a boot on your own, or arrange to be taken out by one of the locals. Don't, whatever you do, forget your entrance tickets.

**Cherangani Hills** (D3): This trekking area northeast of Kitale between the Ugandan border and the Rift Valley is particularly beautiful. It is worth bringing along camping equipment and exploring this area for several days.

**Chiemu Pass** (F5): Probably the most beautiful trip across the lava streams of Tsavo West National Park is from Kilaguni Lodge to Mombasa Road via the untouched Rhino Valley and Chiemu Pass.

**Chyulu Hills** (E5): Verdant, volcanic hills with heavily eroded flanks and lava streams in one of the world's youngest mountain ranges. Located in the West Chyulu Reserve, which borders on Tsavo National Park. As one might imagine, it is a bumpy trip around the approximatley 600 cones.

**Crescent Island Reserve** (E4): A small island in Lake Naivasha where archaeologists recently (1976) discovered scrapers and chisels of obsidian (volcanic rock).

**Crocodile Point** (F5): After crossing the Galana River in Tsavo East National Park, the tourist reaches the beautiful – if not high – Lugard Falls and Crocodile Point. There is a good chance of spotting crocodiles on the sandbanks here.

**Diani Beach** (F6): Here, south of Mombasa, a 135 million dollar tourism project is being implemented. The complex will eventually consist of 26 hotels with 6,500 beds, plus an employees' "city" which will house 40,000. The profusion of signs is shocking, but the few hotels and bungalows which have been built so far are on one of Kenya's most beautiful beaches and need fear no competition in the near future. Diani Beach is at least 10 km (6 miles) long, wide, and protected by coral reefs. Palm trees grow along it, and one can walk from hotel to hotel on the soft, almost white sand. The resort buildings have been imaginatively designed and the splendid displays of flowers in their gardens are a sight for sore eyes. This is how most people imagine an ideal holiday on East

Africa's coast! The hotels (the best-known are Leisure Lodge, Two Fishes and the Robinson Club Baobab) are all close to the Jadini Woods, where flora and fauna still flourish.

**Dodoni Reserve** (G5): This reserve is on the Somalian border south of the Kiunga road.

**East Turkana National Park** (E1): The area (which is still easiest to reach by air) became famous as a result of the prehistoric finds of Richard Leakey, the son of Dr. Louis Leakey. Since these discoveries, East Africa has been accepted as the most probable "cradle" of mankind.

**Eliye Springs** (D2): A pretty, park landscape with gently rolling hills on the western shores of Lake Turkana. The low trees are alive with multi-coloured birds, and termite mounds in bizarre shapes abound. The Eliye Springs Fishing Lodge, next to the springs after which it is named, has a nice bar and a swimming pool.

**Emali** (E5): The turn-off onto the much-used track to Amboseli National Park is here, at this town on the Mombasa Road between Mombasa and Nairobi.

**Embagaai Crater** (D5): It is best to combine a visit to this crater with a trip to Ngorongoro Crater. Both are across the border in Tanzania. The descent into the Embagaai from Windy Gap is very steep, but worthwhile. Herds of gnus and zebras, rhinos and lions, hippos, hyaenas, flamingos and other water birds may be spotted here.

**Embu** (E4): The town is named after the Wa-Embu tribe living in the vicinity. These people are said to be related to the Kikuyus. They farm the foothills of Mt. Kenya, and the town is therefore an important market place and transshipment centre.

**Ferguson's Gulf** (D1): Marvellous angling is possible at this bay north of Eliye Springs on Lake Turkana. There is a modest lodge here and white sand dunes along the shore. About 200 species of bird can be seen in this area, and whoever would like to see more can take a boat to Central Island where flamingos and other birds breed in three small crater lakes.

**Formosa Bay** (G5): This used to be the name of the wide bay on the Indian Ocean into which the River Tana flows (between Malindi and Lamu); today it is called Ngwana Bay.

**Fort Hall** (E4): Starting point in Kikuyu country (previously the White Highlands) for the trip round the Mt. Kenya massif (on the B 20).

**Fort Jesus** (F6): The first Europeans on Kenya's coast, the Portuguese, built this fortress in 1593 to protect their harbour and Mombasa. After some cruel fighting in 1698, the last nine Portuguese in the fortress were overwhelmed by Arabs, who were then able to carry on, undisturbed, their flourishing slave trade from Mombasa. The fort, in the eastern part of the town, is impressive by reason of its size alone: the walls are up to 2.5 m (8 ft) thick and more than 16 m (50 ft) high … and all this perched on a coral reef! Fort Jesus has been a national monument since 1960 and houses a museum that documents the last thousand years of history.

**Fourteen Falls** (E4): These waterfalls on the Athi River lie beyond Thika in Ol Donyo Sapuk National Park. Instead of following the path to the foot of the falls, which drop some 30 m (98 ft), stop halfway and admire the marvellous cascades.

**Galana River** (F5): Starts inland, south of Nairobi, as the Athi and Tsavo Rivers. These two sources join at Tsavo and the Galana River flows into the Indian Ocean at Mambrui, north of Malindi.

**Garissa** (F4): This city on the Tana River is the administrative centre of the northeast province. It has a small airfield and is therefore a good starting point for exploring the area. The border with Somalia is nearby, as are the Arawale Game Reserve and the Tana River Primate Reserve. Cross-country vehicles and experienced safari drivers are needed here.

**Garsen** (G5): A town on the Tana River, at the junction of the road to Lamu (on the coast) and the Garissa-Malindi road. Garsen is also said to be the point at which the Galla take over from the Giriama. The Idsowe Sanctuary is a reserve for herons, which can be found here in large numbers particularly in June and July.

**Gede** (G5): An insignificant place, sometimes mistakenly called Gedi, near the national monument of the same name. Both Gede and the Ruins of Gedi are north of Watamu and can be reached on the road to that park.

**Gedi National Monument** (G5): It wasn't until 1884, as a result of photos by Sir John Kirk, that these ruins of an Arabian city deep in the jungle were rediscovered by the world. In 1927 the government of that day declared Gede a historic monument, but excavations could not begin until 1948, after the site had been made a national park. It is not known why Gede was founded, nor is it known why the inhabitants left: they were, however, obviously in a big hurry. The small museum with a few finds from the site provides no answer to this question. What can still be seen in the "city" are a few mosques and walls, as well as fourteen single-storey houses made of coral blocks which were named for the treasures found in them. These items, which include Indian glass and Chinese porcelain, prove that Gede, a town of about 2,500 inhabitants, was prosperous indeed.

**Gilgil** (E4): Numerous prehistoric finds were made here, near the equator between Naivasha and Nakuru. These are now on display in the Hyrax Hill Museum near Nakuru. The military cemetery at Gilgil is a reminder of the fact that this was the main garrison town of the old colony. Today, the military buildings are used by the Kenyan army, the Salvation Army and the East African postal service.

**Giriama Point** (F6): The most beautiful viewpoint in Shimba Hills Game Reserve is about 500 m (1,600 ft) above sea level in the gently rolling hills south of Mombasa. There is a great variety of flora, and sable antelopes, which are scarcely seen anywhere else in Kenya, were introduced here and have become a speciality of the reserve.

**Hell's Gate** (E4): The "Gate", on Lake Naivasha, is a deep, eroded crack in the rocks over which two rock needles seem to stand guard. It is rather difficult to reach. On peering down, the visitor sees an extremely wide ravine, the walls of which are red-coloured as a result of layers of minerals. The luxuriant vegetation has attracted numerous bird species (at least 400) which can be sighted, given some patience, around the hot springs. An easy path leads down from the two needles to the hot springs.

**Hell's Kitchen** (F5): The rocks of Hell's Kitchen bear similarities to those of Hell's Gate. However, these cliffs north of Malindi, which are up to 30 m (100 ft) high, "shine" in many colours – white and orange, beige to reddish brown.

**Homa Bay** (C4): This is really only a run-down fishermen's village on the eastern shores of Lake Victoria. It lies in a hollow between two pointed cones and is 27 km (17 miles) away from the Lambwe Valley Game Reserve.

**Hyrax Hill** (D4): Several prehistoric finds were made here and a small museum in a converted farmhouse has pottery, tools, pestles and pearls on display. There is an open-air museum at the sites themselves: a mountain fortress from the Iron Age, a settlement consisting of thirteen cave homes, and a cemetery. The women here were buried with all their goods and chattels, but the men were buried without any grave-goods. For the imaginative visitor the skeletons themselves are a source of speculation: most of the dead were buried in a bent position.

**Indian Ocean** (G5/6): It forms Kenya's eastern boundary, a coastline stretching for almost exactly 400 km (250 miles). Except for where rivers flow into the sea, the entire coast is protected by coral reefs. These make it possible to swim out for quite a distance without being exposed to ocean currents or, for example, sharks. Most of the beaches are wide and long, with fine, almost white, coral sand.

**Isinya** (E4): This centre south of Nairobi used to be a Mau-Mau penal colony. It was converted in 1961 into a primary school, an arts and crafts school and an agricultural school, after the drought and flood disasters of 1960 had brought about the deaths of 30% of the Masai in the area and 300,000 head of cattle.

Now, local Masai are taught here, and leather and bead embroidery articles made by them may be bought at "original" prices. Since 1972, a tannery has been part of the complex.

**Isiolo** (E3): This tiny place north of Mt. Kenya is the starting point for visits to the area inhabited by the Turkana. These people, like the Hindus, hold their livestock to be sacred, and thus, a link to their ancestors and their gods.

**Isiolo Game Reserve** (E3): This reserve on the Uasa Nyiro River north of Mt. Kenya occupies an area of 192 sq. km (74 sq. miles). It was united with the Shaba Reserve in 1974, and the Samburu Game Reserve is just across the river.

**Isodwe** (G5): Trips to this heron colony 4 km (2.5 miles) south of Garsen in the Tana delta can be made from Malindi. The best time for a visit is June/July – the heron breeding period.

**Jumba la Mtwana** (F6): The ruins of this slave trading post, dating back to the 14th and 15th centuries, are located north of Nyali and Kenyatta Beach. Although this historic monument is not as impressive as the one at Gede, it is nevertheless of interest. The site, which was overgrown until 1972, has four mosques, three houses and a cemetery. The best-preserved building is the big mosque on the beach.

**Kabete** (E4): The ecclesiastical and academic quarter of Nairobi is located to the northwest of the city centre on the road to Naivasha. Here, the Bible and the prayer book were first translated into the language of the Kikuyu, and the first stone church for these people was built.

**Kaisut Desert** (E2): Marsabit National Game Reserve is in the middle of this desert in northern Kenya. Mt. Marsabit (1,844 m/ 6,050 ft), on which the reserve is located, has a woody, cratered landscape.

**Kakamega Forest** (D3): This area, north of Kisumu on Lake Victoria, is reminiscent of West Africa's rainforests. Animals species – especially big game – are few. By way of compensation, there is a bewildering variety of plant life.

**Kariandusi National Monument** (D4): Dr. Leakey discovered Kariandusi during his second stay in East Africa in 1928. In the unpretentious museum one learns that the spot one is standing on was at one time, 9,500 years ago, beneath 60 m (197 ft) of water. Objects which can be seen here include flints and other splitting instruments made from obsidian, a volcanic rock.

**Kenyatta Beach** (F6): This marvellous sand beach with several good hotels adjoins Nyali Beach north of Mombasa. Here, as is usual along the coast, there are coral reefs offshore, making swimming up to these protective "walls" a harmless pleasure. Suitable for children, too.

**Kericho** (D4): Not surprisingly, Kenya's tea centre is in the middle of the most important tea-growing area. The square in the town centre is called Chai – "tea" – Square, the planters are well off, and the Tea Hotel arranges tours through the young plantations. The first tea shrub was planted here in 1906, and the first plantations were established in 1924.

**Kikambala Beach** (F6): The most northerly holiday beach on the Mombasa coast is 6 km (4 miles) long. Sisal is grown in this area.

**Kikuyu Region** (E4): This area northwest of Nairobi used to be called the White Highlands. The land here is subject to intensive agricultural utilization, the main crops being sisal, pineapples, coffee and tea.

**Kilifi Creek** (F6): This "creek" is really a deep fjord which one must cross by ferry to reach Kilifi. (A Reptile House next to the ferry landing provides a distraction for those faced with a long wait.) The Rare River, flowing into it, forms an expansive lagoon.

**Kilifi** (F6): This town has stayed typically African – nothing exciting, but lively. The Mnarani Hotel, situated above the enchanting bay, is already a popular holiday centre. Kilifi is in the midle of a cashew-growing area; a (Bolognese) factory provides work for 1,500 people. The nuts are packed, ready for eating, and oils used in brake fluid are manufactured from the shells.

**Kilimanjaro** (E5): The highest mountain in Africa (5,896 m/ 19,340 ft) lies in its own nature reserve just over the border in Tanzania. From Masai Amboseli National Park there is, weather permitting, a marvellous view of the snow-capped mountain. Understandably, this is a favourite background for safari photos. Mt. Kilimanjaro has a total of three peaks. The Schira saddle is 4,900 m (16,000 ft) high and is what is left of a crater. The Mawenzi peak is 5,051 m (16,570 ft) and is the laval nucleus of an earlier crater, weather-beaten and eroded. Only experienced mountaineers should attempt this peak! Kibo peak is the highest and youngest part of the volcanic mountain. The usual route up to Kibo summit is from Marangu in Tanzania to the forest region around the Mandera Hut. Then there is a long ascent along the tree line to Horombo Hut in the moorland. Kibo Hut, at 4,700 m (15,420 ft), is only reached on the second day. A strenuous, but not dangerous, climb.

**Kilimanjaro National Park** (E5): The park encompasses Mt. Kilimanjaro above the populated areas.

**Kilindi** (F6): "Place of deep water" is the name of the deep bay which separates Mombasa from the mainland. There is, of course, a ferry connection.

**Kilindi Harbour** (F6): The area around Mombasa's modern, international seaport is a suitable destination for adventure-seeking night strollers.

**Kinangop** (E4): At 3,906 m (12,815 ft) this is the second highest peak in Aberdare National Park. The park, incidentally, is one of the highest in the world.

**Kindaruma Dam:** This impressive piece of engineering on the Tana River was completed in 1965. It has bold, broad curves, a road 1.5 km (about a mile) long on top, and is linked with another, many-branched reservoir. The slopes descending to the river are an ornithological paradise.

**Kinya Ole** (G5): Many hotels and travel agencies in Malindi offer half-day trips to this small island about 50 km (30 miles) away. A lone, happy-go-lucky Englishman has turned the place into a Robinson Crusoe-like island, which paying guests can enjoy. Barbeques and dancing Giriama girls are among the attractions. Caters a bit too much to the tourist trade!

**Kipini** (G5): This small harbour in the east of the Tana estuary is an excellent starting point for trips around the delta or up the Tana River.

**Kisii** (D4): Good hotels are a strong point of this town located in the cultivated hills south of Kisumu near Lake Victoria. Oyugis, on the way to the town, is a breeding ground for pelicans between August and March.

**Kisite** (F6): The most beautiful coral gardens on the East African coast are found at this National Marine Park south of Shimoni on Kenya's southeastern border.

**Kisumu** (D3): After the construction of the long railway line to Uganda, Kisumu was the gateway to Lake Victoria. Although the steamers that now ply the lake have made it considerably less important, it is still considered to be the capital of western Kenya. The suburbs have grown enormously. Of principal interest in the city centre are a number of religious buildings. The heron colony near Kisumu has about 1,000 breeding pairs from March to July.

**Kitale** (D3): This town in western Kenya near the border with Uganda is conveniently situated between Mt. Elgon and Saiwa Swamp National Park. It has an interesting museum (the National Museum of West Kenya) with good natural history and ethnographical collections.

**Kitui** (E4): This town east of Nairobi is the "capital city" of the good-looking Akamba tribe.

**Kora Reserve** (F4): This 1,280 sq. km (495 sq. mile) large game reserve in central Kenya is separated from Rahole National Reserve and Meru National Park by the Tana River. George and Joy Adamson, of "Born Free" fame, worked in this area, and a nearby waterfall was named after them.

**Kuku Plain** (F5): An area of gently rolling bushland between Mount Kilimanjaro and the Chyulu Hills. Characteristic of this part of Tsavo National Park are the lava streams partially overgrown by bushland. Many elephants can be seen here.

**Kwale** (F6): The main entrance to the Shimba Hills Game Reserve is south of Mombasa near the border with Tanzania.

**Lake Baringo** (D3): Only well-known routes should be taken to this lake north of Nakuru in the Rift Valley, as there is danger of becoming bogged down in mud in this area. Cognoscenti enthuse about Lake Baringo Lodge, which is homely but equipped with all modern conveniences, including a swimming pool encircled by a lawn reminiscent of England. It is possible to water-ski and bathe in the lake at no risk, and motor boats navigate between the local hippos to Gibraltar Island, East Africa's biggest goliath heron colony.

**Lake Bogoria Reserve** (D3): The lake, between Nakuru and Lake Baringo, is a genuine alternative for tourists unable to reach the bird paradise of Lake Turkana. Here, there are geysers, pink flamingos… and the Tugs, a Nilotic Hamite tribe whose most famous son is Kenya's president, Arap Moi. In addition, there is a romantic campsite on an island in the lake.

**Lake Chala** (E6): A small lake near the Tanzanian border, 12 km (8 miles) from the border crossing at Taveto.

**Lake Elmenteita** (D4): This lake, southeast of Lake Nakuru, is a soda lake where pink flamingos can be found in abundance. As the land round the lake is cultivated, ploughs are continually bringing prehistoric finds to light.

**Lake Jipe** (E6): A favourite destination among ornithologists and anglers, the lake is located at the foot of Mt. Kilimanjaro on the border with Tanzania. It is about 77 sq. km (30 sq. miles) in size. Westbound travellers from the coast used to head for this lake if they were afraid of crossing Masai country to the north. To the left of the main gate, in Maktau Cemetery, lie the Indians killed during World War I.

**Lake Magadi** (E5): This soda lake, which produces 84,000 t of soda ash each year, is southwest of Nairobi, almost on the Tanzanian border. It is nowhere deeper than 3 m (10 ft) and is frequently populated by flamingos. The scenery around the lake is marvellous.

**Lake Manyara National Park** (D6): This park comprises 314 sq. km (120 sq. miles) south of the Ngorongoro Crater in Tanzania. It boasts a salt lake, swamps, hot springs and savanna as well as forest regions. Lake Manyara Hotel, on the edge of the Rift Valley at the northern end of the lake, is the starting point for hunting trips in the area. From here there is a marvellous view over the lake and the park, which is famous for its "tree lions". In addition, rhinoceroses, elephants and buffalos can be spotted here.

**Lake Naivasha** (E4): This lake in the eastern Rift Valley alters in size depending on the rainfall, and is full of reed islands. Crescent Island – where chisels and scrapers made of obsidian and dating from the Stone Age were found in 1976 – is situated in the lake. Lake Naivasha was discovered in 1883 by the German naturalist/explorer Gustav Fischer, whose party was forced to turn back by the Masai. Until 1902 the province of Naivasha belonged to Uganda. In 1904 the first experimental farm for pigs, sheep, cattle and zebras was set up here.

**Lake Nakuru National Park** (D4): This park, with an area of 200 sq. km (77 sq. miles) is best known for its flamingos, up to two million of which may congregate here at one time. Four hundred other species of bird as well as waterbuck, reedbuck, zebra, impala, Grant's gazelle, lions, leopards, buffalos, hippos and rhinos can also be seen here. The park is 8 km (5 miles) from Nakuru town, northwest of Nairobi.

**Lake Ndutu** (D5): This small salt lake near the Ngorongoro Crater in Tanzania is in the middle of an acacia forest. There is an abundance of bird life here, and a tent lodge for the convenience of avid ornithologists.

**Lake Rudolf** (D/E1): Lake Turkana was originally christened Lake Rudolf in honour of the Austrian archduke who sponsored the explorer – Count Teleki – who discovered it.

**Lake Sindi** (D4): This small (4 sq. km/1.5 sq. miles) crater lake near Kendu Bay on Lake Victoria is rich in bluish-green algae and therefore visited by huge flamingo flocks.

**Lake Turkana** (D/E1): The former Lake Rudolf, 7,680 sq. km (2,965 sq. miles) in size, is tourism's latest discovery: the landscape is photogenic, there is an abundance of animal life (birds, fish), and more than 20,000 crocodiles. The water is clean, and the area – surrounded by volcanic hills – is very hot. Since 1970 the eastern shores have been a national park (East Turkana National Park). On Central Island, numerous flamingos live on three volcanic lakes.

**Lake Victoria** (B/C4): The world's third biggest lake (after the Caspian Sea and Lake Superior) has an area of 69,485 sq. km (26,828 sq. miles). Only the narrow eastern part of the lake belongs to Kenya; the remainder is shared by Uganda and Tanzania. Numerous islands, papyrus swamps, beaches and bays contribute towards its renowned beauty.

The main town on Kenyan soil is Kisumu (originally Port Florence), which was reached by the Uganda railway line on December 20th, 1901.

**Lambwe Valley National Park** (C4): Formerly a reserve, this area was "promoted" to national park status in 1976. Up to now, it has little of interest other than a herd of about 200 roan antelopes.

**Lamu** (G5): Lamu is an island 225 km (140 miles) from Malindi, north of the Tana swamps on the Indian Ocean. As no cars are allowed on the island, visitors must park their vehicles on the banks of the Mokowe and cross the Mkanda Channel by ferry. Being so far off the beaten track, Lamu has retained its Arabian character (there are about 25 mosques!) and gives an impression of what other towns and islands on Africa's east coast must once have looked like. Unfortunately, the enchanting town of Lamu was almost completely destroyed by fire in 1982. Reconstruction work is proceeding slowly, which is a pity as a trip to Lamu used to be an unforgettable experience. The doors with wood carvings are famous, and are said to show more motifs than those in Zanzibar. In earlier times, "thrones" made of ebony with inlaid bone or ivory were manufactured here. Teak trunks and model dhows are on offer. There is an interesting museum here.

**Lemagrut** (D5): This impressive mountain in the crater highlands of Tanzania is 3,188 m (10,460 ft) high. It is situated between Lake Ndutu and Lake Mangara south of Ngorongoro Crater.

**Lenana** (E4): The most accessible of the three peaks of Mt. Kenya massif is 4,985 m (16,355 ft) high. Although it could be called the "tourist" peak it should, like the other peaks of Mt. Kenya, be treated with respect. It is advisable to ascend Lenana in the company of experts. The ascent takes four to five days, and it is possible to overnight at huts belonging to the Mountain Club of Kenya.

**Likoni** (F6): A small town separated from Mombasa by Kilindi Bay, but linked to the city by a ferry. Although the ferry trip takes only four minutes, the wait can be a long one... Of interest in this otherwise characterless town is the Likoni Holiday Resort, a children's holiday home established by Sir Ali bin Salim (the British guardian of the coast from 1922 to 1931) which is still said to operate at cost.

**Limuru** (E4): Because of its excellent, healthy climate, Limuru was put forward as the capital of Kenya. By way of compensation for the fact that Nairobi was given that honour, Limuru received a beautiful golf course, two hotels offering marvellous cuisine, and a hunting club. Important sources of income here are tea, coffee, pyrethrum and a shoe factory. Two places worth recommending: Farm Hotel, 2 km (1 mile) outside town; and Kentmere Club, with its old-fashioned, cosy rooms (black ceiling beams, open fireplaces) and excellent cuisine.

**Lolokwe** (E3): The scenery around this high mountain (2,000 m/ 6,560 ft) in the north of Samburu Reserve is worth seeing.

**Longonot** (E4): This active volcano near Lake Naivasha can – and should – be visited on a day-trip from Nairobi. A well-marked but slightly strenuous footpath goes right round the edge of the crater

(2,803 m/9,196 ft). The village of Longonot is not worth seeing, but the acacia trees (new plantations in part) are.

**Loyangalani** (E2): The "place of trees" is a starting point for boat trips to the bird paradise of South Island in Lake Turkana and for excursions through the interesting countryside nearby. The Molo Bay area features bubbling hot springs and colonies of flamingos, cormorants, pelicans, ibis and cranes.

**Lugard's Falls** (F5): These falls, in Tsavo East National Park, are not very high, but impressive. The water tumbles down from a crack in a small, pink, brown and yellow plateau.

**Machakos** (E4): The sole attraction of this town on the Mombasa Road is a clock tower which was erected in honour of Princess Margaret on the occasion of her visit in October 1956. Thanks to the missionary Stuart Watt, the area is able to live quite comfortably from fruit plantations and jam factories.

**Mackinder's Camp** (E3/4): The ascent to Point Lenana begins here. In the vicinity, just before Nenyuki, the road crosses the equator.

**Malindi** (G5): Once a small Arabian settlement – which Vasco da Gama "visited" in 1498 and renamed after his wife – Malindi today is a popular resort. On its northern beach there are modern hotels with swimming pools, the latter being necessary because the ocean water here is discoloured. Natural deposits in the Galana River, which enters the Indian Ocean at Sabaki, turn the water a "dirty red". Malindi is a particular favourite with men travelling alone. The hotels have their own gardens – colourful contributions to the beauty of the coast. A 7 m (22 ft) high monument to Vasco da Gama was unveiled (much to the chagrin of nationalist-minded Africans) in 1960, but is no longer in good repair. Of more interest is the building in the background, a good example of the architecture of the colonial period (1890), tastefully set off by African plants with marvellous blossoms.

The old part of Malindi is located round the simple Bohra mosque. Although there are no architectural highlights in this quarter, the atmosphere is "genuine African".

Juma's mosque, with its cupolas and pinnacles, may only be entered by Moslems. Up until 1873, slave trading was carried on here on Fridays.

The first recorded reference to Malindi dates back to the 13th century; for years the city was Mombasa's adversary. In the 16th century, splendid sultans' houses adorned the streets, but the town was later abandoned and went to ruin. From 1861 to 1890 the slave trade flourished. Today the town, which creates a distinctly sleepy impression, lives from the tourist trade, from the brewing of "Tembo" (a palm beer) and from fishing. Tourism has been encouraged since 1965 and presently provides employment for 45% of the population. To the south of Malindi there are some holiday beaches

(e. g. Silver Sands) with hotels and pretty camping sites. Adjoining Malindi is **Malindi Marine National Park.** The Easterbrook snake collection, in natural-looking surroundings, is worth a visit.

**Mambrui** (G5): This sleepy town 13 km (8 miles) north of Malindi dates back to the 15th century. Of particular interest here is a column-supported tomb with Chinese porcelain vessels from the Ming dynasty (6½ of the original 10 remain). The Riadha mosque, built in 1962, towers over the village.

**Manda:** (G5): A half-finished (or destroyed?) bastion and the ruins of Takwa, dating from the 16th or 17th century, are worth seeing on this island next to Lamu. The ruins were excavated in 1851 and 1972 and are scattered over 5 hectares. For adventure seekers and archaeology buffs, there are various other sites to explore, including the town of Manda itself. The access route is unusual, to say the least: you have to wade through mangrove swamps.

**Maralal Reserve** (E3): Maralal itself, the principal town in the area of this reserve in central Kenya, is on Lorogi plateau, at a height of 1,987 m (6,520 ft).

**Marsabit Mountain** (E2): This mountain in the Kaisut Desert is 1,844 m (6,050 ft) high, with woods and crater lakes.

Marsabit gained world fame through the elephant Ahmed, who was painted by David Shepard, filmed by John Huston and placed under the special protection of Kenya's president. In 1974 this "state" elephant died at the early age of 55. Since then the stream of visitors to the national park has slowed down. The semi-desert, with its thick scrub and withered trees, is interesting because of the odd groups of basalt rocks. Experts believe them to have served ritual purposes, but the natives themselves are of the opinion that they were used by the British for defence in the war...

**Masai Amboseli National Park** (E5): As this is the most popular of Kenya's national parks, it should definitely not be missed. The Masai administer 128 sq. km (50 sq. miles) of the park, which have been set aside for them and their herds. A large variety of wildlife can be seen here, including elephants, rhinos, buffalos, lions and cheetahs. From Amboseli Park, one has a breathtaking view of Mt. Kilimanjaro.

**Masai Mara Reserve** (D4): Said by those who ought to know to be the best game reserve Kenya still has! An unforgettable experience during big game migrations.

**Mau Forest** (D4): This huge forest, northeast of Kericho on the way to Nakuru, has hardly been explored.

**Mawenzi** (E5): Second highest Kilimanjaro peak (5,051 m/16,570 ft) should only be attempted by experienced mountaineers. The peak was formed by the laval nucleus of a crater.

**Mayer's Farm** (E4): The owners of this cattle farm, 2,230 hectares in size, have opened their property to visitors. The farm extends from the edge of the Rift Valley far into it. Of unique beauty are the gardens, which are kept a luxuriant green by warm springs. The huts of Masai who live here can also be visited. A bit "touristy", but it does convey an impression of Masai customs.

**Menengai** (D4): The "place of corpses" is a crater 89 sq. km (34 sq. miles) in area and up to 483 m (1,585 ft) deep. Masai warriors who fell in an important battle (said to have taken place in 1854) lie here. In this battle, the Masai from Naivasha finally triumphed over those from Laikipia. Volcanic vapours rise out of the crater, where wild animals of the savannas, e. g. giraffes, live.

**Meru** (E3): A small town on the northeast spurs of the Mt. Kenya massif, Meru is surrounded by thick woods and brush. The oak trees here are famous in East Africa. Meru's museum contains an interesting folklore collection, which is, however, somewhat strangely laid out. Visitors interested in the lives of bees will find informative exhibitions.

**Meru National Park** (F3): This park should not be confused with Mount Meru Game Reserve west of Mt. Kilimanjaro in Tanzania. Special attractions here include black rhinos, which have been re-introduced in the area. Prehistoric finds show that they were originally part of the animal population here. Because of the 15 rivers (full of crocodiles!), mosquito nets and malaria prophylaxis are indispensable! A particularly nice spot is Leopard Rock Safari Lodge on Murera River.

**Mida Creek** (G5): This broad lagoon south of Malindi (and the Gedi and Watamu excavations) is protected by a long headland and has several islands. The trip from the south to the western part of Mida Creek is particularly scenic. There is an abundance of bird life in this area.

**Mnarani** (F6): The departure point of the rickety, but safe, ferry which crosses Kilifi Creek is on the south side of the inlet. The ferry runs round the clock, crossing to Kilifi in four minutes. There is a small mosque, built in 1970, and a good hotel high above the rocks. From November to April bird-watching trips can be taken into the mangrove swamp. Bramwells is before the ferry, the ruins of Mnarani after it.

**Mokowe** (G5): This is the departure point for the crossing to Lamu as well as for trips along the Tana River. The direct route (little traffic) from Mokowe via Bodhei to the river also leads to Arawala Game Reserve, which was created specifically to protect Hunter's antelopes along the Tana.

**Molo** (D4): Lamb and the Highlands Hotel have made this town south of Kericho well known.

**Mombasa** (F6): East Africa's most important port and Kenya's second largest city has a population of about 350,000. It is situated, to a large extent, on a coral rock island at the meeting point of two deep, long lagoons. Consequently, it is almost completely surrounded by water. To the north it is linked with the mainland by a bridge over Mombasa Harbour; to the south a ferry plies Kilindi Harbour; to the west both a road and a railway bridge connect the island to the coast.

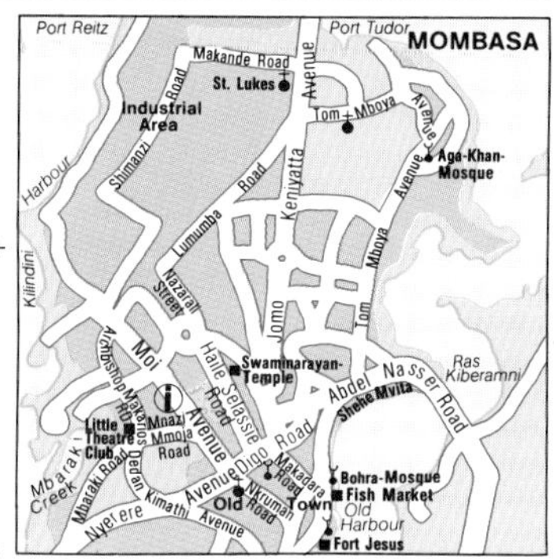


More than 200 years of Arabian trade have left their stamp on Mombasa. Two Portuguese forts, as well as Fort Jesus (1592), bear witness to the significance of this city down through the centuries. Of course, the Arabian slave trade flourished here until it was abolished in the second half of the 19th century. At the beginning of the 20th century the town gained importance again as a result of the construction of the railway line to Uganda.

In spite of the cosmopolitan atmosphere and strong Arabian influence, the charm typical of Africa is not missing here, and this makes for a delightful mixture. The old part of the town, east of Digo Road, has narrow alleyways and (in part) dilapidated houses. New Mombasa has wide, modern avenues, such as Kilindi Road, the main business street. The symbol of Mombasa – four outsize white tusks – along with souvenir shops and a tourist information office, are located along this bustling thoroughfare. At Christmas, at least, dhows arrive at the old port from the Orient, laden with carpets and pewter wares. The new Kilindi Harbour was constructed to be a modern international port and is linked by the railway line to Lake Victoria.

The wide (four-lane) highway from the airport to the city is naturally named after Jomo Kenyatta. A favourite meeting place in town is the wide terrace of the Castle Hotel on Kilindi Road, where pedlars often hawk souvenirs. Opposite the hotel, Msanifu Combo Road leads to the Home Industry Centre, with its excellent range of goods on offer.

Worth seeing, if not really spectacular, are the fish market early in the morning and, if only to put an end to the myth of pitching and rolling dhows, the old port. Earlier, when these ships were still a significant means of transport, they could indeed be seen here, taking refuge from the monsoons (for instance, in the bad month of March).

Great Britain and the Sultan of Zanzibar, Agha Khan, contributed towards the polytechnical college, which was inaugurated in 1951 as the Mombasa Institute of Muslim Education. It can be recognized by its rich ornamentation, and is found beyond the Port Tudor cliffs to the northeast of the city. On the other side of Tom Mboys Avenue is the Agha Khan mosque.

As far as international entertainment goes, a popular choice is the Hotel Oceanic, which has had a casino since 1972. Mombasa Yacht Club is particularly elegant: visitors can become members for the duration of their stay. Guests are also welcome at Mombasa Golf Club.

**Mombasa Road:** The 480 km (300 mile) long highway stretches from the end of the Uhuru Highway, at Nairobi, to Mombasa. It splits Tsavo National Park into East and West.

**Moshi** (E6): This town, south of Mt. Kilimanjaro and east of Arusha in Tanzania, (altitude: 813 m/2,667 ft) is the centre of a coffee growing district. It also has a special attraction: the big mosque, built in 1956–57, has the Islamic confession of faith on the outside – in English!

**Mount Elgon National Park** (D3): This national park, on the border with Uganda, is 169 sq. km (65 sq. miles) in size. Mount Elgon (4,230 m/13,878 ft), at its centre, is extremely interesting and has an impressive crater 8 km (5 miles) in diameter and 610 m (2,000 ft) deep.

From Labot, one can travel by jeep to a mountain hut at 3,650 m (11,975 ft), and from there it is an easy climb to the rim of the crater. The El Goni caves on the slopes of Mount Elgon are worth seeing.

**Mount Kenya** (E4): Kenya's highest mountain is located northeast of Nairobi in the national park which bears its name. The massif consists of three peaks – Batian, with 5,199 m (17,057 ft); Nelion, with 5,188 m (17,021 ft); and Lenana, with 4,985 m (16,355 ft) – and occupies an overall area of about 400 sq. km (154 sq. miles). The mountain, which rises directly from savannas and farmland, has 32 lakes and 15 glaciers.

The Kikuyu worship the "White Mountain" as the residence of their god, Mwene-Nyaga. Only Lenana peak is suitable for tourists with little alpine experience, and then expert guidance is a must. There is a well-trained mountain rescue service in the park.

**Mount Meru** (E5): Mount Meru Game Sanctuary in Tanzania is not to be confused with Meru National Park northeast of Nairobi. Mt. Meru is 4,566 m (14,980 ft) high, and can be ascended from Okokola.

**Mpunguti:** See Kisite.

**Mtwapa Creek** (F6): Tours can be taken around this deep fjord north of Mombasa. There are mangrove swamps here and also the **Kenya Marineland and Snake Park,** an oceanarium 4,065 hectares in size. Feeding times are 11 a. m. and 4 p. m., and the animals can be watched from an underwater observation post. The park is accessible via Kenya Marinas, and the route is well marked.

**Murang'a** (E4): The former Fort Hall is at the foot of Mt. Kenya on the Nairobi side. Its name is sometimes spelled Maranga or Muranga. A site above the village is considered holy by the Kikuyu, who are supposed to have originated here with the union of Gikuyu and Mumbi.

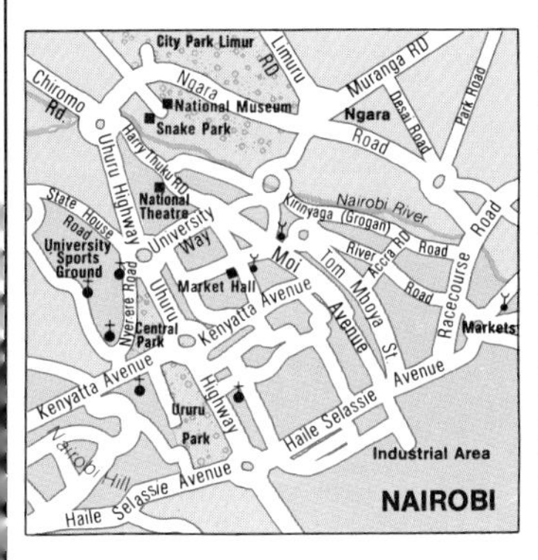


**Mzima Springs** (E5): At sunset many animals come to water at these springs in Tsavo West National Park. Even without the wildlife, Mzima oasis is a marvellous natural spectacle. It is also a fascinating geological phenomenon: day after day 227 million litres (55 million gallons) of water bubble up out of the dry lava plain. This water gathers underground 40 km (25 miles) away from the Chyulu Hills, puts in an appearance here at Mzima, and disappears into the ground again before flowing into the Tsavo. Mombasa's water comes from this source; thus, that city probably has the country's cleanest water.

**Nairobi** (E4): Kenya's capital and biggest city has a population of more than 830,000 and a municipal area of 689 sq. km (266 sq. miles).

In 1899 the site was chosen as construction headquarters for the Uganda railway on account of its favourable climate. The city is at the foot of the Mount Kenya massif, at an altitude of 1,660 m (5,446 ft). It was named after the rivulet Ngara Nairobi, which means "cold water" in the language of the Masai. In the early days, corrugated steel huts formed a kind of "Wild West" settlement, the location of which delighted the British. Eventually, they took over the entire highlands area, naming it the White Highlands. In 1907 Nairobi became the capital of British East Africa: after the foundation of the independent republic of Kenya in 1963, it retained that status.

Today, Nairobi is a mixture of Europe and Africa, with wide, flower-lined boulevards, parks, skyscrapers and an impressive traffic system. A confident, bustling metropolis; not surprisingly, East Africa's most important centre of trade.

The modern Kenyatta Conference Centre offers, together with the neighbouring hotels, excellent conference facilities. The business district consists principally of Moi

Avenue, Muingi Mbningu Street, Kenyatta Avenue and Mama Ngina Way.

The relatively young town has very few places of historical interest, but the national museum, with a good natural history and an outstanding folklore collection, is significant. Nairobi National Park is generally recognized as the "best" sight.

Useful, and free, are the "Nairobi Handbook" (appears once a month) and "What's On".

Like Mombasa, Nairobi has an Uhuru Park on a slope above the downtown area. From here one has an excellent view of the City Square. The inside of the Parliamant buildings (which can be visited on request) are worth seeing, as is a performance at the Donovan Maule Theatre, said to be the best in the whole of East Africa. The Hilton, opposite the information office, is the optical centre of Nairobi, but the 28-storey Kenyatta Conference Centre reaps far more superlatives: it is Kenya's highest building, has the biggest rotating restaurant in the country, and boasts the world's second biggest conference hall.

**Nairobi National Park** (E4): See chapter "National Parks and Game Reserves".

**Nakuru** (D4): The country's third largest city is northwest of Nairobi, at an altitude of 1,800 m (5,905 ft), and has a population of approximately 60,000. It is the most important transshipment centre for agricultural produce. A source of particular pride is the super-modern station, where the Uganda railway branches off to Lake Victoria.

**Namanga** (E5): This border post was previously the starting point for excursions to the Tanzanian national parks, some of which are now accessible again. Inquire before setting out to avoid disappointment. The entrance to Masai Amboseli National Park (and Game Reserve) is in the vicinity.

**Nanyuki** (E3): This village in the foothills of Mt. Kenya (altitude: 1,966 m/6,450 ft) is the main starting point for trips into Mt. Kenya National Park: the ascent, with guide and porters, is organized by Naro Moru River Lodge. The Silverbeck Hotel here was famous for its Equator Bar, which burned down in 1974.

**Narok** (D4): The main village in the Masai district is 150 km (93 miles) west of Nairobi at an altitude of 1,905 m (6,250 ft). The tall Nilotic Hamites live here, and one can purchase beadwork made by local Masai women at the filling station.

**Naro Moru** (E4): For many mountaineers the "River Lodge" is the last preparation post before conquering Mt. Kenya. There are cosy little houses and a camping site here as well.

**Nelion Peak** (E4): See "Mount Kenya". The ascent of Nelion peak should only be attempted by mountaineers with alpine experience and in top physical fitness.

**Ngobit** (E4): A hamlet in a wooded valley on Ngobit River, Ngobit is an angler's paradise. Trout were released in the rivers of the Aberdares as early as 1905. The stretch where angling is most likely to be successful is some 20 km (12 miles) long.

**Ngomeni** (G5): This excellent natural harbour is north of Malindi and Mambrui on a narrow headland. Since 1966 the Italians have had their equatorial rocket-firing base here. Ngwana Bay (formerly Formosa Bay) is full of little mangrove islands and sand banks.

**Ngong Hills** (E4): Nairobi's mountains look like huge humps and reach an altitude of 2,458 m (8,064 ft). They are venerated by the Masai. Because of the abundance of wildlife here, the game reserve (see chapter "National Parks and Game Reserves") was set up in 1961.

**Ngorongoro Crater** (D5): The crater is situated in Ngorongoro Conservation Area, a Tanzanian national park which covers 6,500 sq. km (2,510 sq. miles). It is up to 600 m (1,968 ft) deep, and has a diameter of 20 km (12 miles). The rim of the crater is wooded, and in the depression itself there are swamps, acacia forests, grasslands, bush and a salt lake. The best view of the crater is from Windy Gap: the steep track into it from here should only be tackled in a crosscountry vehicle.

There are landing strips for Ngorongoro Crater at Ndutu, and between Windy Gap and Crater Lodge. Accommodation is available at Ngorongoro Crater Lodge, Ngorongoro Wildlife Lodge, Ndutu Tented Lodge and, right on the edge of the crater, Dhillon's Lodge. Camping in the crater itself is possible only with special permission, if at all; but there is a camp site near Crater Lodge. Land Rovers can be rented; it is advisable, however, to take part in excursions organized by the lodges. The marked tracks may not be left.

The animal life in the crater is fascinating: elephants, lions and leopards, black rhinos and zebras, giant forest hogs, buffalos, hartebeests, gnus, waterbucks, Thomson's and Grant's gazelles, bushbucks, elands, Masai giraffes, servals, spotted hyenas, bat-eared foxes, and various types of jackal.

**Nyahururu Falls** (E4): Kenya's third biggest waterfall (75 m/246 ft) used to be called Thomson's Falls after the well-known Scottish explorer (after whom Thomson's gazelles are also named). The high-altitude training camp for Kenyan athletes is located directly above the falls at the Thomson's Falls Lodge (altitude: 2,400 m/7,874 ft).

**Nyali** (F6): Mombasa's "garden suburb" is located on the coast north of Mombasa Harbour. The villas here are all privately owned, so there isn't much to visit. There are, however, several hotels and a golf course for hotel guests.

**Nyali Beach** (F6): Modern hotels offering numerous sports facilities characterize this popular beach on Mombasa's northern coast. Nearby Frère Town was one of the first places where liberated slaves settled. The bell of Emmanuel Church is said to have tolled every hour throughout the night when slave dhows were in sight. In the church vestry hangs a painting of Matthew Wellington: freed from slavery by the British, he accompanied Dr. Livingstone until his death and even brought the explorer's mummified body back to Zanzibar.

**Nyeri** (E4): The "secret capital" of the Kikuyus is not particularly exciting, but two famous hotels – "Treetops" and "The Ark" – are found here. Some seasoned travellers claim that a stay in one of these is the highlight of a visit to Kenya. Lord Baden-Powell, the founder of Boy Scouts and Girl Guides, is buried near here.

**Oldeani Plateau** (D6): German and South African settlers tilled this rich farmland between Ngorongoro Crater and Lake Manyara from the end of the First World War until World War II.

**Ol Donyo Sapuk or Sabuk** (E4): There is an incredible panoramic view from this area, which was made a national park in 1969. One can see as far as Mt. Kenya and the lakes in the Athi River plain. The park itself is interesting because of the forest stock and variety of bird life.

**Olduvai Gorge** (D5): A sandy track leads from the main road to an interesting prehistoric excavation site here, northwest of Ngorongoro Crater in Tanzania. The gorge became world famous as a result of excavations carried out by the British anthropologists, Louis and Mary Leakey.

**Olorgesailie National Park** (E4): Dr. Leakey and his wife made important prehistoric finds here from 1942 onwards. The objects excavated are presumed to be from 4 to 500,000 years old. Camping is possible in the national park, or visitors can stay overnight in little cottages (own food supplies). A small museum opened here 1975.

**Ol Tukai** (E5): The hotels of the Masai Amboseli Game Reserve are found in Ol Tukai, which owes its existence to the U. S. film company, Paramount. The first huts were erected here for the film team making "The Snows of Kilimanjaro"; later the buildings were presented to the Masai.

**Oyugis** (D4): Between August and March, this town near Lake Victoria is a breeding-ground for pelicans.

**Poacher's Look-out** (E5): A vantage point near Chyulu Gate in Tsavo West National Park.

**Rahole Reserve** (F3): This reserve is opposite the Kora Reserve on the northern side of the Tana River.

**Ramisi:** This sugar refinery was founded as early as 1927 and presently employs more than 3,000 people. It is located in the midst of the largest sugar cane plantations, and produces about 15,000 t of white sugar annually.

**Rift Valley:** The East African Rift Valley extends from the Dead Sea to Beira, covering a total distance of 6,500 km (4,040 miles). In Kenya it resembles a 700 m (2,300 ft) deep gash running from Lake Turkana in the north to the Tanzanian border in the south. Nairobi lies to its east. The numerous lakes in the valley are thought to be the remains of a huge, landlocked sea. The almost vertical walls of the valley are up to 80 km (50 miles) apart. Excursions from Nairobi to the floor of the Rift Valley are popular.

**Roaring Rocks** (E5): From these cliffs near Mzima Springs in Tsavo West National Park, there is an outstanding view of the surrounding countryside.

**Robinson Island** (G5): Kinya Ole, only 2.5 sq. km (one square mile) in size, is known by tourists as Robinson Island. Here, one can dive, swim, or simply laze around and enjoy the grill parties instituted by the entrepreneur behind this "shipwreck" paradise, a certain David Hurd.

**Ruiru** (E4): A turbine driven by water from a small dam near Ruiru provided the first electric power to Nairobi in 1906. Otherwise, the town is known as the site of Sir and Lady McMillan's 8,000 hectare ranch. Famous guests at the ranch include Winston Churchill and Theodore Roosevelt.

**Sabaki** (G5): The Galana River enters the Indian Ocean here, depositing on Malindi's beaches the red sand of Tsavo. Because of the reddish water, most tourists in this area prefer the swimming pools at their hotels to the beach.

**Sagana** (E4): The road round Mt. Kenya intersects the B5 to Nairobi at Sagana, an important stop on the way to Meru National Park.

**Saiwa Swamp National Reserve** (D3): This is virtually the only place in Kenya where one can be certain of seeing the rare Sitatunga (marshbuck). There are more than a thousand of them in this park, which was established in 1972 and is only 191 hectares in size.

**Samburu-Isiolo Shaba Game Reserve** (E3): See "National Parks and Game Reserves".

**Satima** (E4): This peak in Aberdare National Park is 3,999 m (13,120 ft) high.

**Serengeti National Park** (D5): Tanzania's biggest national park became famous throughout the world as a result of the film "Serengeti Must Not Die". The park is 12,950 sq. km (5,000 sq. miles) in size and borders on the Kenyan Masai Mara Reserve in the north. Its position between Lake Victoria and Tanzania's crater highlands ensure widely varied landscape: lakes and grasslands, savannas and gallery forests, granite hills and volcanic rubble.

**Shaba Game Reserve** (E3): See chapter "National Parks and Game Reserves". So far this region to the northeast of Mt. Kenya has hardly been developed at all.

**Shanzu** (F6): This holiday resort is located on the wide, flat, fine-sand beach to the north of Mombasa.

**Shimba Hills Game Reserve** (F6): The bare tops of the hills in this reserve near the east coast are crowned by Borassus palm trees.

**Shimo la Tewa Sports Centre** (F6): In 1976 the African Safari Club opened this sports centre near Mombasa in the converted gardens of a villa from the colonial period. Every conceivable sports facility is available here, but water sports, including deep-sea diving and fishing, are first in popularity.

**Shimoni** (F6): As might be expected, the "place of caves" features numerous caves with stalactites and bats. More important, from the tourist's point of view, is the Kisite-Mpunguti Marine National Park, which was set up in 1973 just in time to save the coral world of the reef off Shimoni and the four coral islands in front of it.

**Shitani Flow** (E5): "Devil's" flow is a wide, fairly young lava stream 8 km (5 miles) long, which has pushed its way from the Chyulu Hills far into the plain. Klipspringers can almost always be seen here.

**Snake Park** (E4): African and Asiatic snakes and reptiles can be seen in this famous park in Nairobi.

**Sokoke-Arabuku Forest** (F6): This coastal forest is 40 km (25 miles) from Kilifi.

**Subukia Valley** (D4): Intensively cultivated land of volcanic origin is found here, between Nakuru and Nyahururu. Rocky wooded ravines characterize the southern end of this lovely valley.

**Taita Hills** (F6): The hills, often referred to as Kenya's Switzerland, contrast strongly with the surrounding landscape. Taita Hills Lodge, on one of the hilltops, is famous; it was built in 1973, at the same time as the architecturally marvellous Salt Lick Lodge in Tsavo West National Park.

**Takaungu** (F6): This lonely, fishermen's village, north of Mombasa between Vipingo and Kilifi, is worth visiting. It is 5 km (3 miles) from the coast road.

**Takwa** (G5): The 16th and 17th century ruins on Manda Island, next to Lamu, are an officially recognized monument. They are surrounded by lush, coastal jungle.

**Tana River:** The 1,200 km (750 mile) long Tana has its source near Meru and flows in a wide arc towards the Indian Ocean. At the coast, it forms a big swamp area and a delta between Malindi and Lamu.

Today the river is Kenya's largest source of (hydro) electric power.

**Tana River Primate Reserve** (G5): See chapter "National Parks and Game Reserves".

**Tarangire National Park** (D6): Tanzania's second biggest national park is 12,000 sq. km (4,633 sq. miles) in size and is located south of Lake Manyara. The park is relatively young; consequently, the wild animals are still somewhat shy. Elephants, black rhinos, lions, leopards, cheetahs, greater and lesser kudus, zebras, buffalos, gnus, waterbucks, impalas and elands can be seen here. The vegetation is varied, and includes gallery forests and swamps, thorn scrub, and dry savanna.

**Tewa Underwater Caverns** (G5/6): The caves, south of Watamu, are populated with giant bass and of interest to experienced divers.

**Tharu Desert** (F5): The first travellers to the dry and lonely area between Mariakni and Voi in Tsavo National Park gave it this name.

**Thika** (E4): Possibly the main attraction of this town northeast of Nairobi is the nostalgic-looking Blue Post Hotel, reminiscent of the days when authoress Elspeth Huxley travelled – albeit arduously – here. Today Thika is a noisy industrial town with textile and paper mills, tanneries, and fruit-canning factories.

**Thomson's Falls** (E4): See "Nyahururu Falls".

**Tiwi Beach** (F6): Accommodation is mainly in bungalows at this popular holiday beach to the south of Mombasa.

**Treetops** (E4): This hotel in Aberdare National Park became world famous in 1952: England's Queen (then Princess) Elizabeth was staying here on February 5th when she received the news of her father's death and her consequent ascension to the throne. The wooden hut of those days has long since given way to an 80-bed hotel with a restaurant. Advance booking for this expensive pleasure is absolutely necessary.

**Tsavo National Park** (E/F5): Much of Kenya's biggest national park (20,567 sq. km/7,940 sq. miles) has purposely been left in a wilderness state. Tsavo East, for example, is virtually undeveloped and may only be entered with special permission. Tsavo West is famous for its scenic beauty: lava streams, Mzima Springs, etc. There are 60 mammal species, 400 bird and 1,000 plant species to be marvelled at here. More elephants and black rhinos are found in this area than anywhere else in the world. Of particular interest as far as accommodation goes are: Kilanguni Lodge, Taita Hills Lodge and Salt Lick Lodge.

**Tudor Creek** (F6): The creek separates Mombasa from the mainland in the northeast, and becomes Mombasa Harbour.

**Turtle Bay** (G6): There are numerous possibilities for water sports at this popular beach on the northern coast near Watamu. As in most coastal areas, the beach is protected by coral reefs.

**Uaso Nyiro River** (E3): The so-called "Brown River" separates the two game reserves, Samburu and Isiolo: the vegetation along it is luxuriantly tropical.

**Voi** (F5): The gate to Tsavo East National Park is at the end of the Tharu Desert (heading towards Nairobi) on the Mombasa Road. In World War I, Voi was an important railway junction (troop transport). Between the police station and the African Inland Church is a soldier's cemetery.

**Wajir** (G2): Collectors may have heard of this city in northeastern Kenya because of its swords in red-dyed, camelskin scabbards. The place has a definite Arabian air, with whitewashed houses, palm trees, and camels in the alleyways. The once-famous, splendid Royal Yacht Club (!), in a shiplike building in the middle of the desert, has become run down as the African Mgamia Camel Club.

**Wasini** (F6): This coral island is on the southern coast between Shimoni and Kisite-Mpunguti Marine National Park.

**Watamu** (G6): Up until now, this village between the Indian Ocean, Gedi and Mida Creek has remained typically African: craftsmen's huts and small shops in a clearing. Unfortunately, souvenir dealers are threatening to gain the upper hand. The nearby Watamu Beach Hotel – with a view of the numerous small islands in the beautiful bay – is extremely popular (especially among bachelors).

**Watamu Marine National Park** (G6): This is the south corner of the Marine National Reserve, which extends as far as Malindi National Park.

**West Chyulu National Reserve** (E5): This chain of wooded volcanic hills, 389 sq. km (150 sq. miles) in size, borders on Tsavo West National Park.

**White Highlands** (E4): The fertile, gently rolling countryside northeast of Nairobi is the centre of Kikuyu land. Coffee, tea, sisal and pineapples are cultivated in this region.

**Windy Gap** (D5): The best view of Ngorongoro Crater in Tanzania is from Windy Gap: it is also possible, though the way is extremely steep, to descend into the crater from here.

**Yatta Plateau** (F5): This lava stream, possibly the world's longest, extends from the north into Tsavo National Park. It runs, more or less parallel to Mombasa Road, for 300 km (190 miles) and is a mere 2 km (1.2 miles) wide.

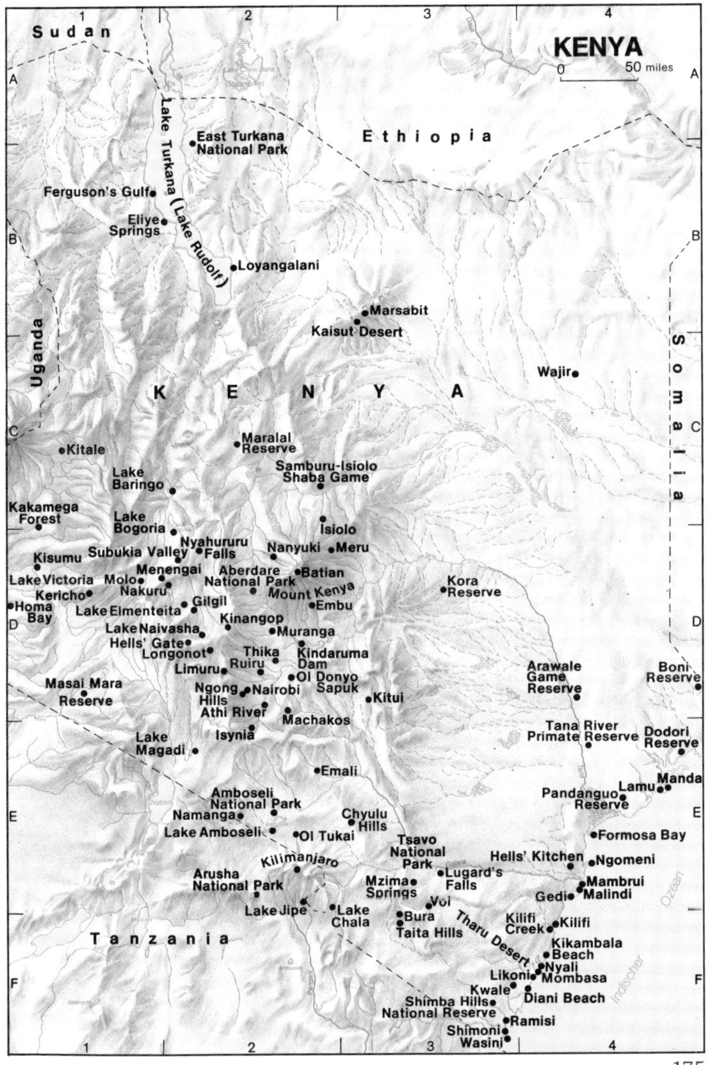
KENYA
0 50 miles
Sudan
Ethiopia
Uganda
Somalia
Tanzania
KENYA
Lake Turkana (Lake Rudolf)
East Turkana National Park
Ferguson's Gulf
Eliye Springs
Loyangalani
Marsabit
Kaisut Desert
Wajir
Maralal Reserve
Kitale
Samburu-Isiolo Shaba Game
Lake Baringo
Kakamega Forest
Lake Bogoria
Isiolo
Kisumu
Subukia Valley
Nyahururu Falls
Nanyuki
Meru
Menengai
Aberdare National Park
Batian
Lake Victoria
Molo
Nakuru
Mount Kenya
Kora Reserve
Kericho
Gilgil
Embu
Homa Bay
Lake Elmenteita
Kinangop
Lake Naivasha
Muranga
Hells' Gate
Longonot
Thika
Kindaruma Dam
Limuru
Ruiru
Ol Donyo Sapuk
Arawale Game Reserve
Boni Reserve
Masai Mara Reserve
Ngong Hills
Nairobi
Kitui
Athi River
Machakos
Tana River Primate Reserve
Dodori Reserve
Lake Magadi
Isynia
Emali
Lamu
Manda
Pandanguo Reserve
Amboseli National Park
Namanga
Chyulu Hills
Lake Amboseli
Ol Tukai
Formosa Bay
Tsavo National Park
Hells' Kitchen
Ngomeni
Kilimanjaro
Arusha National Park
Mzima Springs
Lugard's Falls
Mambrui
Malindi
Gedi
Lake Jipe
Lake Chala
Voi
Bura
Taita Hills
Tharu Desert
Kilifi Creek
Kilifi
Kikambala Beach
Nyali
Likoni
Mombasa
Kwale
Diani Beach
Shimba Hills National Reserve
Ramisi
Shimoni
Wasini
Indischer Ozean

# Useful Information

## Currency

The standard monetary unit of Kenya is the shilling (KSh) divided into 100 cents. For current rates of exchange, see the separate fold-out map.

## Currency Control

Kenyan currency may not be imported or exported.

There is no limit on the amount of foreign currency which may be imported, but this must be declared (in duplicate) on a "Currency Declaration Form" on arrival in Kenya. The visitor retains a copy of this form and all transactions made while in Kenya must be recorded on it. In order to change Kenyan shillings back into a foreign currency, proof of the original exchange and of subsequent transactions must be produced. It is therefore recommended that all receipts be retained.

Only banks and certain hotels are authorized to change money. It is illegal to buy or sell Kenyan currency on the black market.

Most foreign currencies (U. S. dollars are probably the best bet) will be accepted in Kenya – either as banknotes or traveller's cheques.

## Traveller's Cheques, Credit Cards

Well-known credit cards and traveller's cheques are accepted in Kenya. Again, you might find it easier if traveller's cheques are made out in U. S. dollars.

## Entry Formalities

On arrival, visitors' passports are stamped with a visitors' pass valid for a specified period. Visas are not required from citizens of the Commonwealth (with the exception of Nigerian, Australian and Sri Lankan citizens, and British passport holders from India, Pakistan and Bangladesh). Visitors from most western European countries do not need a visa either. US citizens need a visa in order to enter Kenya, as do any visitors who have been to South Africa.

As requirements are often changed at short notice, we would advise you to check on your status before finalising holiday arrangements. Applications for visas should be made at least 30 days before departure and addressed to a Kenyan Embassy or Consulate (or to a British Embassy if Kenya has no diplomatic representative in a particular country).

High Commission of the
Republic of Kenya
45 Portland Place
London, W1N 4AS
Tel. (01)6 36 23 71

Mission of Kenya to the U. N.
866 United Nations Plaza
Room 486
New York, N. Y. 10017
Tel. (2 12)4 21 47 40

High Commission of the
Republic of Kenya
6th Floor
Andahl House

33–35 Ainsley Avenue
Canberra, A. C. T. 2600
Tel. (0 62)47 47 88

High Commission of the
Republic of Kenya
415 Laurier Avenue East
Ottawa
Tel. (6 13)5 63 17 73

Once in Kenya, applications for extension of stay should be addressed to the Immigration Department, Bima House, Harambee Avenue, Nairobi.

**Departure Tax**
On leaving Kenya every visitor pays an airport tax of US$ 10.

**Customs**
Visitors of seventeen years and over may bring the following goods duty free into Kenya:

- cameras, movie cameras, film and binoculars for their own use;
- 250 gms of tobacco (in the form of cigarettes, cigars, pipe tobacco, etc.)
- 1 litre of spirits or wine
- ½ litre of toilet water and perfume

Personal effects are of course exempt from duty. Duty must be paid on gifts. No firearms, drugs or obscene literature may be brought into Kenya.

**Health and Medical Care**
Only visitors arriving in Kenya from an area infected with yellow fever need vaccinations and are asked to produce a vaccination certificate.

Malaria prophylactics are recommended, the course of tablets beginning two weeks before arrival in Kenya, covering the duration of your stay and continuing two weeks after departure.

Although it is safe to swim in the sea and in swimming pools, you should resist the temptation to take a dip in lakes, rivers, etc. (or to drink the water!) because of the danger of infection from schistosome parasites.

Medical care is good. There are well-equipped hospitals and pharmacies (especially in Nairobi and Mombasa) with highly-trained personnel. Your hotel or travel agent will be able to assist you if you need medical attention. Emergencies in the bush are dealt with by the Flying Doctor Service. Most tour operators subscribe to this service but if this is not the case you would be well advised to do so yourself. Temporary membership is not expensive and the service guarantees free air transport from anywhere in Kenya to a medical centre. The headquarters of the Flying Doctor Service are in Nairobi (P. O. Box 30125, Tel. 50 13 01). Ask your travel agent or a representative of the Kenyan Tourist Office for more information.

**Language**
Swahili and English are official languages. English is spoken in all major tourist centres.

**Accommodation**
A good range of hotels in Nairobi and along the coast. Prices vary greatly depending on facilities,

whether you choose full board, bed and breakfast, etc.

In the national parks and game reserves accommodation is in lodges and tented lodges. A Kenyan invention, the range of lodges available offer everything from simple but adequate accommodation to luxurious cottages. They all enjoy beautiful surroundings and are the ideal way to observe Kenya's animals in their natural environment.

Campsites are also to be found in the parks and reserves and along the coast. Some are inaccessible if weather conditions are poor so make enquiries beforehand. (Some people worry about being exposed to wild animals, but in fact theft is a far greater problem! Take care not to leave valuables in your tent.)

**Electricity Supply**
240 volts, 50 cycles A. C. 2-pin round or 3-pin square plugs. Hotels and lodges will provide adaptors for 220 and 110 volt appliances.

**Clothing**
Along the coast, beachwear is acceptable in hotels as well as on the beach but for walking around town, light cotton dresses, shirts, etc. should be worn. On safari, traditional cotton safari suits afford protection from sun and dust. Remember to pack some warmer clothing for evenings in the bush, especially at higher elevations. In Nairobi, lightweight clothes are suitable all year, but for the cooler months of July and August you might well be glad of something a little warmer.

**Opening Hours**

**Banks:** Monday to Friday 9 am–1 pm (in some case 8.30 am–12.30 pm). Saturdays 9 am–11 am.

**Shops:** Generally speaking, 8.30 am–5 pm during the week. Closed for lunch between 1 pm and 2.30 pm.

Souvenir shops often have longer opening hours, and shopping is sometimes possible on Sundays and national holidays.

**National Holidays**
January 1st; Good Friday; Easter Monday; May 1st; June 1st (Madaraka Day); October 20th (Kenyatta Day); December 12th (Independence Day); December 25th and 26th; Idd-Ul-Fitr (the end of Ramadan, as decreed).

**Tipping**
As a general rule, porters should receive a tip of 2 Ksh. In restaurants service is often included in the bill. As taxis do not have meters you will have to agree on a price anyway.

**Diplomatic Representation**
A Kenya Tourist Office or your travel agent should be able to give you the address of your embassy or consulate in Kenya. We would advise you to keep the address and telephone number handy in case of any kind of problem – loss of passport, damage to personal effects, etc.

British High Commission
Bruce House
Standard Street

Nairobi
P. O. Box 30465
Tel. 33 59 44

American Embassy
Moi-Haile Selassie Avenue
Nairobi
Tel. 33 41 41

Canadian High Commission
Comcraft House
Haile Selassie Avenue
Nairobi
Tel. 33 40 33

Australian High Commission
Development House
Moi Avenue
Nairobi
P. O. Box 30360
Tel. 33 46 66

**Information on Kenya**

Kenya Tourist Office
60 East 56th Street
New York, N. Y. 10022
Tel. (2 12)4 86 13 00

Kenya Tourist Office
9100 Wilshire Boulevard
Doheny Plaza Suite 111
Beverley Hills, Ca. 90121
Tel. (2 13)2 74 66 35

Kenya Tourist Office
13 New Burlington Street
London W1X 1FF
Tel. 01 8 39 44 77

There is no Kenya Tourist Office in either Canada or Australia at the present time.

# Travelling in Kenya

In Swahili "safari" simply means to travel. Thus, whatever you do in Kenya, if you leave your beach hotel for it, you can say you're going on safari....

The whole country is served by a close network of small airlines, from which you can, if the need arises, charter a whole plane (could be worthwhile if several persons have the same goal). Otherwise, the airlines offer tours with pilots acting as guides, or trips to specific destinations. Standards are high, the planes well-maintained, and the pilots are very reliable. And costs of charter are reasonable. The most important airline companies, apart from the international Kenya Airways, are Air Kenya, Safari Air Services, Caspair and Boskovic Air Charters in Nairobi, and Air Kenya and Malindi Air Services in Mombasa and Malindi. Every travel agent, as well as your hotel management in Kenya, will have information on the flights available.

If you're not in a hurry, travelling by train in Kenya can be a marvellous experience. Tourists often like to try the Mombasa – Nairobi line. The first-class compartments are inexpensive and clean, and the train restaurants and bars can be recommended. If you travel at night you lose out on the marvellous views, but you do the long haul in your sleep.

At every station passengers are greeted by dealers offering fruit, vegetables and other refreshments, some (roasted ants, for example) more exotic than others!

Only the really tough, adventure-seeking souls should try a cross-country bus journey. You might well decide that such a journey is worthwhile, however, as nowhere more than here will you come into such close contact with Kenyans. A regular bus service operates between Mombasa and Nairobi, the trip taking around seven hours. When buses arrive in town, each passenger is dropped off in front of his own home. Time-consuming, but a nice idea...

Group taxis, which link all the fairly big towns and set off when full, only cost a little more. Without a doubt, travelling by group taxi also falls in the adventure category – the way the taxis are driven may well take your breath away!

Most people who have experience of travelling in Kenya advise against driving a rented car yourself. Better to pay for a driver as well, who not only has to look after the car, but also knows his way about in the usually difficult terrain.

It's also worth bearing in mind that "traffic etiquette" varies from country to country. You may find Kenyan roads – and sidewalks! – more hectic than those you are used to.

# Selected Bibliography


Andreas Fedders and Cynthia Salvadori, *Peoples and Cultures of Kenya,* Transafrica, Nairobi, Rex Collings, London 1979

Graham Hyslop, *Musical Instruments of East Africa I: Kenya,* Nelson, London 1975

John Jewell, *Dhows at Mombasa,* East African Publishing House, Nairobi 1976

Keith David Jones, *Shepherds of the Desert,* Elm Tree Books, London 1984

John D. Kesby, *The Cultural Regions of East Africa,* London, New York, San Francisco 1977

Joseph Ki-Zerbo, *Histoire d'Afrique Noire,* Librairie Hartier, Paris 1978

Eike Haberland, *Galla Süd-Äthiopiens,* Stuttgart 1963

*Schwarz-Afrikaner,* ed. Walter Raunig, Pinguin Verlag, Innsbruck 1980

*A Cultural Atlas of Africa,* ed. Jocelyn Murray, Phaidon, Oxford 1981

Basil Davidson, *Africa in History,* Paladin Books, London 1974

Basil Davidson, *Africa in Modern History,* Penguin Books, London 1978

Uwe Schlegelmilch, *Die Suaheli,* München 1983

Robert L. Tigmor, *The Colonial Transformation of Kenya,* Princeton Univ. Press, Princeton, New Jersey 1976

Kenya
*The following denominations are currently in use:*

| | | |
|---|---|---|
| Notes: | Shillings | 100, 50, 20, 10, 5 |
| Coins: | Shillings | 1 |
| | Cents | 50, 10, 5 |

**Please note:**

Every effort was made to ensure that the information given was correct at the time of publication.

However, as it is not possible for any travel guide to keep abreast of all changes regarding passport formalities, rates of exchange, prices, etc., you are advised to contact the appropriate authorities (embassy, bank, tourist office ...) when planning your holiday.

The publishers would be pleased to hear about any omissions or errors.

# Contents

## Personal Notes

Personal Notes

## Personal Notes

**Personal Notes**

**Personal Notes**

**Personal Notes**

**Personal Notes**

**Personal Notes**